Making the Internet Profitable for You

Jeremy Lopez

Making the Internet Profitable for You

Published by Dr. Jeremy Lopez

Copyright © 2023

ENDORSEMENTS

Jeremy does an excellent job of giving balanced instruction on how to meditate, and also explaining the benefits that come from having a regular meditation and mindfulness practice. I love how Jeremy is not afraid to learn from and quote those outside the Christian tradition. He is able to explain the ancient concepts simply from a Biblical perspective. – Kari Browning, Director, *The Beautiful Revolution*

You are put on this earth with incredible potential and a divine destiny. This powerful, practical man shows you how to tap into power you did not even know you had. – Brian Tracy – Author, *The Power of Self Confidence*

I found myself savoring the concepts of the Law of Attraction merging with the Law of Creativity until slowly the beautiful truths seeped deeper into my thirsty soul. I am called to be a Creator! My friend, Dr. Jeremy Lopez, has a way of reminding us of our eternal 'I-Am-ness' while putting the tools in our hands to unlock our endless creative potential with the Divine mind. As a musical composer, I am excited to explore, with greater understanding, the infinite realm of possibilities as I place fingers on my piano and whisper, 'Let there be!' – Dony McGuire, Grammy Award winning artist and musical composer

Jeremy dives deep into the power of consciousness and shows us that we can create a world where the champion within us can shine and how we can manifest our desires to live a life of fulfillment. A must read! – Greg S. Reid – *Forbes* and *Inc.* top rated Keynote Speaker

I have been privileged to know Jeremy Lopez for many years, as well as sharing the platform with him at a number of conferences. Through this time, I have found him as a man of integrity, commitment, wisdom, and one of the most networked people I have met. Jeremy is an entrepreneur and a leader of leaders. He has amazing insights into leadership competencies and values. He has a passion to ignite this latent potential within individuals and organizations and provide ongoing development and coaching to bring about competitive advantage and success. I would highly recommend him as a

empowered and have strong faith that God has indeed given us these Bible-based Universal and Divine Laws to tap into so that we can live and create an abundant life. – Constance Arnold, M.A., Author, Speaker, Professional Counselor, Host of *The Think, Believe & Manifest Talk Show*

TABLE OF CONTENTS

Introduction

In the vast landscape of the 21st century, the Internet stands as a sprawling network that connects billions of people across the globe. It has revolutionized the way we communicate, work, and entertain ourselves. However, amidst this sea of digital connectivity lies an unprecedented opportunity—a chance to turn the Internet into a profitable venture that can transform your life.

So, welcome to *Making the Internet Profitable for You*, a book designed to guide you through the intricate pathways of the online world, revealing the secrets to harnessing its immense potential. Whether you're an aspiring entrepreneur, a budding freelancer, or simply someone seeking to enhance your financial prospects, this book is your compass to navigate the digital marketplace and unlock unprecedented opportunities for success.

As technology continues to advance at an astonishing pace, traditional business models are being disrupted, and new paradigms are emerging. The Internet has become the ultimate equalizer, giving individuals the ability to compete on a global scale, regardless of their background or resources. With the right knowledge, tools, and strategies, you can carve out your own niche, tap into lucrative online markets, and build a sustainable income stream.

In this book, we will embark on a transformative journey together, delving into the principles, tactics, and techniques that will empower you to thrive in the ever-evolving digital landscape. From understanding the fundamentals of online entrepreneurship to identifying profitable niches, from leveraging social media platforms to harnessing the potential of e-commerce, we will leave no stone unturned in our quest to make the Internet work for you.

Drawing from the expertise of seasoned professionals, industry leaders, and successful digital entrepreneurs, *Making the Internet Profitable for You* provides you with a comprehensive roadmap to capitalize on the boundless opportunities that the online world presents. We will explore various business models, revenue streams, and marketing strategies that have proven to be effective in driving profitability and sustainable growth.

However, this book is not solely focused on monetary gains. It is about leveraging the Internet to create a life of freedom, flexibility, and fulfillment. It's about cultivating digital skills, building meaningful connections, and embracing the entrepreneurial spirit that thrives in the virtual realm. By unlocking the potential of the Internet, you have the power to design a life on your own terms, where work and passion seamlessly merge.

Are you ready to embark on this transformative journey? Get ready to embrace the digital revolution and harness its immense potential. *Making the Internet Profitable for You* is your guide to turning the Internet into a catalyst for success, helping you shape a future where the boundaries of possibility are defined only by your imagination. Let's dive in and unlock the extraordinary possibilities that await you in the digital realm.

Before we delve into the strategies and techniques that will pave the way for your online success, it's crucial to understand the foundations of the digital economy. In this book, we will explore the key drivers and trends shaping the online landscape, giving you a comprehensive understanding of the immense potential that lies within your grasp.

We will discuss the transformative power of e-commerce and how it has revolutionized the way we buy and sell products and services. From the rise of online marketplaces to the emergence of dropshipping and digital storefronts, we will explore the diverse avenues for generating revenue in the digital marketplace.

Additionally, we will shed light on the gig economy and the flourishing world of freelance work. With the proliferation of remote work and the gig economy's rapid growth, individuals now have unprecedented opportunities to monetize their skills and expertise, breaking free from the traditional constraints of the nine-to-five job.

Understanding the fundamental shifts in consumer behavior and the evolving expectations of the digital consumer is also vital. We will explore the rise of influencer marketing, the power of customer reviews, and the importance of cultivating a strong online presence to build trust and credibility in the eyes of potential customers.

Now that you have a solid foundation in the workings of the digital economy, it's time to unleash your online potential. In this chapter, we will delve into the mindset and skill set required to thrive in the digital realm.

We will discuss the importance of cultivating a growth mindset and embracing continuous learning and adaptation. The online world is ever-changing, and to stay ahead of the curve, you need to be open to new ideas, technologies, and strategies.

Building your personal brand will also be a key focus in this book. We will explore the elements that contribute to a compelling personal brand and how you can leverage it to stand out in a crowded marketplace. From crafting your unique value proposition to building an authentic online presence, we will equip you with the tools to make a lasting impression.

In the online world, effective marketing is the lifeblood of success. In this chapter, we will dive deep into the vast landscape of digital marketing, equipping you with the knowledge and skills to navigate its complexities.

We will explore the power of social media marketing and how you can leverage platforms such as Facebook, Instagram, and LinkedIn to reach your target audience, build a loyal following, and drive traffic to your online ventures.

Search engine optimization (SEO) will also be a focal point, as we uncover the strategies to optimize your online presence and rank higher in search engine results. From keyword research to on-page optimization and link building, we will demystify the world of SEO and empower you to improve your visibility and attract organic traffic.

Now that you have built a strong foundation and acquired the essential skills, it's time to monetize your online presence. In this chapter, we will explore various avenues for generating revenue and turning your digital ventures into profitable enterprises.

We will delve into the world of affiliate marketing, where you can earn commissions by promoting products and services from other companies. We will discuss the strategies for choosing the right affiliate programs, building an audience, and maximizing your earning potential.

E-commerce will also take center stage, as we explore the steps to set up and optimize your online store. From choosing the right products and implementing effective pricing strategies to creating a seamless customer experience, we will guide you through the intricacies of running a successful e-commerce business.

We will focus on scaling your online business and taking it to new heights. We will explore strategies for expanding your reach, increasing your revenue, and solidifying your position in the digital marketplace.

We will delve into the world of automation and delegation, discussing how you can streamline your operations and free up your time by automating repetitive tasks and outsourcing non-essential activities. This will allow you to focus on high-value tasks that drive growth and innovation.

Furthermore, we will explore the concept of strategic partnerships and collaborations. By forming alliances with like-minded entrepreneurs or complementary businesses, you can tap into new markets, share resources, and leverage each other's strengths to achieve mutual growth.

We will also discuss the importance of data-driven decision-making. With the wealth of information available in the digital realm, we will guide you on how to collect and analyze data to gain valuable insights into customer behavior, market trends, and areas for improvement. By leveraging data, you can make informed decisions that optimize your business performance and fuel your expansion.

Lastly, we will touch upon the topic of personal and professional development. As you scale your online business, it's crucial to continuously invest in your skills, knowledge, and personal growth. We will explore strategies for staying ahead of the competition, adapting to industry changes, and nurturing your entrepreneurial spirit.

As we come to the end of this book, you will have embarked on a transformative journey through the intricacies of making the Internet profitable for you. You will have gained insights into the digital economy, mastered essential skills, and uncovered strategies for monetizing your online presence.

Remember, success in the digital realm is not guaranteed overnight. It requires persistence, adaptability, and a willingness to embrace change. But armed with the knowledge and tools presented in this book, you have the foundation to navigate the dynamic landscape of the online world and carve out your own path to success.

The Internet is a vast playground of opportunities waiting to be explored. Whether you choose to launch your own e-commerce store, become a successful freelancer, or venture into affiliate marketing, the possibilities are endless. It's time to step into your digital potential, harness the power of the Internet, and turn your dreams into reality.

Your digital success story begins now. Embrace the challenges, seize the opportunities, and unlock the extraordinary potential that lies within the vast realm of the digital marketplace. The Internet is yours for the taking—make it profitable for you.

In the ever-connected digital landscape, your online reputation holds significant value. In this book, we will explore the importance of building and maintaining a positive online reputation that fosters trust and credibility among your target audience.

We will delve into the world of online reviews and testimonials, understanding how they can impact your business and influence potential customers. You will learn strategies to encourage positive reviews and address negative feedback in a constructive and proactive manner.

Additionally, we will discuss the power of social proof and how leveraging testimonials and case studies can enhance your reputation and attract new customers.

Managing your online presence goes beyond reviews. We will delve into the realm of social media and the impact it has on your reputation. You will discover strategies for crafting engaging social media content, interacting with your audience, and managing potential reputation crises. By building a strong and consistent online presence, you can cultivate a positive reputation that sets you apart from the competition.

In the digital age, innovation and disruption are constant companions. To remain relevant and competitive, you must embrace the ever-evolving landscape and adapt to new technologies and trends. In this book, we will explore the importance of innovation and how it can drive growth and success in your online endeavors.

We will discuss the concept of continuous improvement, encouraging you to seek out new ideas, experiment with emerging technologies, and stay ahead of the curve. You will learn strategies for fostering a culture of innovation within your online business, empowering your team to think creatively and embrace change.

Furthermore, we will delve into the world of emerging technologies such as artificial intelligence, virtual reality, and blockchain. Understanding the potential applications of these technologies will enable you to identify new opportunities and leverage them to gain a competitive edge in the digital marketplace.

Building a profitable online business is not just about short-term gains—it's about sustaining long-term success. In the fnal chapter, we will explore strategies for achieving sustainability and ensuring the longevity of your online ventures.

We will discuss the importance of building a loyal customer base and fostering customer loyalty through exceptional service and personalized experiences. You will learn techniques for nurturing customer relationships, implementing effective customer retention strategies, and maximizing customer lifetime value.

Additionally, we will explore the significance of staying adaptable and agile in the face of industry and market changes. We will discuss the concept of continuous learning and how it can fuel your growth and innovation. By staying informed, embracing new technologies, and adapting your strategies, you can navigate through challenges and position yourself for long-term success.

Remember that success in the online world is a continuous journey. It requires dedication, resilience, and a commitment to ongoing learning. Embrace the opportunities, adapt to changes, and always strive for innovation. The digital marketplace is a vast and dynamic realm, filled with possibilities for those who dare to pursue them.

As you embark on your journey to profitable online success, keep in mind that your mindset and determination are essential. Stay focused, believe in your abilities, and embrace the challenges that come your way. With the right strategies, a strong online reputation, and a commitment to sustainable growth, you have the power to shape your own destiny in the digital world.

So, go forth and seize the opportunities that await you. Make the Internet your ally, your platform for success, and your gateway to a profitable and fulfilling future. Your journey begins now— embrace it and let your online dreams become a reality.

The Digital Landscape

In an interconnected world where information flows freely, ethical practices are more important than ever. In this book, we will explore the significance of ethical conduct in the digital realm and how it can positively impact your online business.

We will discuss the importance of transparency and honesty in your online interactions. Upholding ethical standards in your marketing, customer interactions, and business operations will not only build trust with your audience but also differentiate you from competitors who engage in questionable practices.

Furthermore, we will delve into the realm of data privacy and security. With increasing concerns about data breaches and online privacy, it is crucial to prioritize the protection of customer information and comply with relevant regulations. We will explore best practices for data security, informed consent, and responsible handling of user data.

In the pursuit of profitability, it is essential not to overlook your own well-being. In this book, we will explore strategies for achieving a healthy work-life balance in the digital age.

We will discuss the potential pitfalls of constant connectivity and the importance of setting boundaries between work and personal life. You will learn techniques for managing your time effectively, prioritizing self-care, and avoiding burnout as you navigate the demands of an online business.

Additionally, we will explore the benefits of building a supportive network and seeking collaboration with like-minded individuals. Connecting with fellow entrepreneurs, joining communities, and engaging in mentorship opportunities can provide valuable support, guidance, and a sense of belonging in the digital realm.

As you embark on your journey, remember that profitability is not the sole measure of success. It is equally important to find purpose and meaning in your online endeavors. By aligning your passions and values with your business pursuits, you can create a meaningful impact in the lives of others and make a difference in the world.

Embrace the opportunities, challenges, and constant evolution of the digital landscape. Stay committed to continuous learning, adapt to changes, and strive for excellence in all that you do. The Internet holds boundless potential, waiting for you to harness it and shape your own profitable and purposeful future.

So, go forth with confidence, integrity, and a sense of purpose. Make the Internet a platform for not only financial success but also personal fulfillment and positive impact. Your journey to a profitable and purposeful future starts now—embrace it and let your digital endeavors become a catalyst for the extraordinary.

In today's interconnected world, the internet has transformed the way we live, work, and communicate. It has become a vast digital landscape brimming with opportunities for individuals and businesses alike. One of the most compelling aspects of this digital realm is its potential for profitability. This chapter explores the various avenues available to harness the internet's power and outlines the challenges that come along with it.

The rise of e-commerce and online marketplaces has revolutionized the way goods and services are bought and sold. From small businesses to multinational corporations, the internet has opened up new avenues for entrepreneurs to reach customers across the globe. Setting up an online store or leveraging existing platforms like Amazon, eBay, or Shopify provides a cost-effective way to showcase products, increase brand visibility, and tap into a vast consumer base. However, amidst the vastness of the digital marketplace, businesses face challenges such as competition, maintaining customer trust, and adapting to rapidly evolving technologies.

Advertising and marketing have shifted significantly in the digital age. The internet offers targeted advertising options, allowing businesses to reach specific demographics and tailor their messages accordingly. Platforms like Google Ads, social media advertising, and influencer marketing have become indispensable tools for promoting products and services. Nevertheless, the increasing prevalence of ad-blockers, ad fatigue, and the need to navigate through a crowded digital space pose challenges to marketers. Maintaining creativity, personalization, and providing genuine value to customers are key factors for success in the digital advertising landscape.

The democratization of content creation has empowered individuals to share their skills, expertise, and creativity with the world. Whether through blogging, vlogging, podcasting, or social media, content creators can attract audiences and monetize their work. Platforms like YouTube, Patreon, and Twitch enable content creators to generate income through advertisements, sponsorships, subscriptions, or donations. However, standing out among the vast sea of content and consistently delivering high-quality material remains a challenge. Creators need to find their niche, engage with their audience, and adapt to changing algorithms and viewer preferences.

The internet generates an enormous amount of data every second, providing businesses with unprecedented insights into customer behavior, market trends, and performance metrics. Leveraging data analytics and artificial intelligence, companies can optimize their operations, enhance customer experiences, and drive profitability. However, concerns about data privacy, security breaches, and the ethical use of data continue to be critical challenges in the digital landscape. Striking a balance between leveraging data and protecting user privacy is essential for sustainable growth.

In the digital realm, building trust and maintaining a positive reputation are paramount. Online reviews, ratings, and customer feedback heavily influence consumer decisions. Providing excellent customer service, fostering transparent communication, and addressing concerns promptly are essential for cultivating trust in the digital space. Moreover, businesses must be prepared to navigate crises effectively, as negative incidents can spread rapidly across social media and impact reputation significantly.

The digital landscape is in a constant state of evolution. New technologies such as blockchain, augmented reality (AR), virtual reality (VR), and the Internet of Things (IoT) continue to reshape the digital ecosystem and present fresh opportunities for profitability. Businesses that stay agile, embrace innovation, and adapt to emerging trends will be best positioned to thrive in this ever-changing landscape.

The internet offers an abundance of opportunities for profitability, but it also presents challenges that require careful consideration and adaptation.

Embracing e-commerce, leveraging digital advertising, monetizing content, harnessing and leveraging data, building trust and reputation, and staying abreast of evolving technologies are key strategies for success in the digital landscape.

As technology continues to advance, the potential for generating revenue on the internet will only grow. Innovations like artificial intelligence, machine learning, and automation provide opportunities for businesses to streamline processes, enhance customer experiences, and optimize their operations. By leveraging these technologies, businesses can increase efficiency, reduce costs, and ultimately drive profitability.

Furthermore, the internet offers a global marketplace, allowing businesses to expand their reach beyond traditional boundaries. With the ability to connect with customers worldwide, companies can tap into new markets, diversify revenue streams, and capitalize on emerging trends. The internet's accessibility and interconnectedness make it easier than ever to target specific demographics, customize offerings, and deliver personalized experiences to consumers.

However, amidst the vast opportunities, there are also challenges to navigate. The digital landscape is highly competitive, requiring businesses to differentiate themselves and provide unique value propositions. Standing out among the noise requires creativity, innovation, and a deep understanding of target audiences. Additionally, as the digital space evolves, businesses must continuously adapt to changing algorithms, consumer preferences, and technological advancements. Staying informed and agile is crucial to remaining relevant and competitive.

Data privacy and security concerns are also critical considerations in the digital landscape.

As businesses collect and utilize vast amounts of data, it is essential to prioritize user privacy and protect against data breaches. Implementing robust security measures, adhering to data protection regulations, and being transparent about data usage build trust with customers and ensure long-term sustainability.

The internet offers a wealth of opportunities for profitability, but it requires careful navigation and adaptation to overcome the associated challenges. By embracing e-commerce, digital advertising, content monetization, data-driven decision-making, and focusing on building trust and reputation, businesses can capitalize on the potential of the digital landscape. With a proactive approach, continuous innovation, and a customer-centric mindset, businesses can thrive in the ever-evolving digital world.

In the dynamic digital landscape, businesses must stay agile and continually explore new avenues for generating revenue. Here are some additional strategies to consider:

Offering subscription-based services or products can provide a steady stream of recurring revenue. By providing exclusive content, access to premium features, or regular deliveries, businesses can create a loyal customer base and generate reliable income.

Partnering with other businesses or influencers through affiliate programs can be a lucrative way to earn commissions. By promoting products or services and earning a percentage of each sale referred, businesses can leverage the existing audience and trust of affiliates to drive revenue.

Sharing knowledge and expertise through online courses, webinars, or consulting services can be highly profitable. Many individuals and businesses are willing to pay for valuable insights and guidance in various fields. Creating and selling educational content tailored to specific niches can be a lucrative opportunity.

Collaborating with other brands or influencers to create sponsored content or partnerships can provide a source of revenue. By aligning with relevant brands and reaching their audience, businesses can increase brand exposure, attract new customers, and generate income through sponsored collaborations.

Creating and selling digital products, such as e-books, templates, software, or online tools, can be a scalable and cost-effective way to generate revenue. These products can be distributed instantly, eliminating the need for physical inventory and shipping.

For creative projects, non-profit organizations, or social causes, crowdfunding platforms provide an opportunity to generate revenue through public contributions. By presenting a compelling story or project, businesses can appeal to individuals' generosity and receive financial support.

If a business has unique intellectual property, such as patents, trademarks, or copyrighted materials, licensing those assets to other businesses can generate additional income. This strategy allows others to use or sell products based on the licensed intellectual property in exchange for royalty fees or upfront payments.

Hosting virtual events, conferences, or webinars can be a profitable way to connect with audiences and monetize knowledge or expertise. By charging admission fees, offering sponsorships, or selling merchandise during these events, businesses can generate revenue while delivering value to attendees.

Remember, the digital landscape is constantly evolving, and new opportunities may emerge. It is crucial to stay informed, keep an eye on industry trends, and be willing to adapt and innovate to capitalize on emerging revenue-generating strategies.

By diversifying income sources and exploring various avenues for profitability, businesses can mitigate risks and create a sustainable and resilient digital presence. new revenue streams and optimizing existing ones.

To continue generating revenue in the digital landscape, businesses should focus on ongoing innovation, optimization, and adaptation. Here are some additional strategies to consider:

With the increasing use of smartphones and mobile devices, optimizing your online presence for mobile users is crucial. Ensure that your website, e-commerce platform, and digital content are mobile-friendly, responsive, and provide a seamless user experience across different devices.

Voice assistants and smart speakers have gained significant popularity, changing the way people search for information and make purchasing decisions. Optimizing your content and website for voice search queries can help you reach a broader audience and improve your chances of appearing in voice search results.

Identify specific niches or market segments that align with your products or services. By tailoring your offerings and marketing strategies to target these niche markets, you can differentiate yourself from broader competitors and develop a loyal customer base.

In addition to utilizing data for internal purposes, explore opportunities to monetize your data assets. Anonymized and aggregated data can provide valuable insights for market research, industry analysis, or targeted advertising campaigns. Just ensure that you comply with privacy regulations and gain explicit consent from users.

Expand your presence on online marketplaces by exploring new platforms or expanding into international marketplaces. This allows you to tap into a wider customer base, increase brand exposure, and potentially access new distribution channels.

If your business is suitable for the subscription model, consider creating subscription boxes or curated packages. By offering a recurring delivery of specialized products or experiences, you can provide convenience and personalized offerings to your customers while ensuring consistent revenue.

Collaborate with influencers or micro-influencers in your industry to promote your products or services. Influencer marketing can help you reach a wider audience, build brand credibility, and drive sales. Ensure that you choose influencers whose values align with your brand and target audience.

Explore the potential of VR and AR technologies to enhance customer experiences, particularly in industries such as retail, tourism, or real estate. By allowing customers to virtually try products, visualize spaces, or engage with interactive experiences, you can differentiate your offerings and create additional revenue streams.

Engage with your customers consistently through social media, email marketing, or loyalty programs. Encourage repeat purchases, referrals, and upselling opportunities by providing personalized recommendations, exclusive discounts, or rewards for customer loyalty.

Seek strategic partnerships or collaborations with complementary businesses. By combining resources, expertise, or audiences, you can create mutually beneficial opportunities for cross-promotion, co-creation, or joint ventures that expand your customer reach and revenue potential.

Remember, staying ahead in the digital landscape requires a proactive mindset, a willingness to experiment, and a customer-centric approach. Continuously monitor market trends, engage with your audience, and adapt your strategies based on feedback and insights. By embracing innovation and optimizing your revenue-generating efforts, you can thrive in the ever-evolving digital ecosystem.

Monetizing Your Online Presence

In today's digital age, the internet offers a plethora of opportunities to turn your online presence into a profitable venture. Whether you're a content creator, a small business owner, or an aspiring entrepreneur, understanding how to monetize your online presence is crucial for long-term success. This chapter will provide you with a comprehensive guide to harnessing the power of the internet and maximizing your earning potential. I wanted to include this chapter within the book to offer a few practical strategies that I've used over the years to build Identity Network into one of the leading resource sites in the world.

Identify your passion, expertise, or unique perspective that sets you apart from others. Focusing on a specific niche will help you attract a targeted audience, which is essential for monetization.

Develop high-quality, engaging content that resonates with your target audience. Whether it's through blog posts, videos, podcasts, or social media, consistently provide valuable and relevant content to build a loyal following.

Craft a strong brand identity that reflects your values and resonates with your audience. Consistency in visuals, tone of voice, and messaging will help establish trust and recognition among your followers.

Utilize ad networks like Google AdSense to display targeted advertisements on your website, blog, or YouTube channel. Earn revenue based on clicks or impressions generated by your audience.

Collaborate with brands relevant to your niche to create sponsored posts, videos, or social media content. Ensure transparency and authenticity to maintain your audience's trust.

Partner with companies and promote their products or services through unique affiliate links. Earn a commission for every sale or conversion generated through your referrals.

Share honest reviews and recommendations of products or services you genuinely endorse. Build credibility and trust with your audience, increasing the likelihood of conversions.

Set up an online store to sell physical products related to your niche. Utilize platforms like Shopify or WooCommerce to streamline the selling process.

Create and sell digital products such as e-books, online courses, templates, or software. Leverage platforms like Gumroad or Teachable to handle payments and distribution.

Offer premium or exclusive content to your audience through a membership site or subscription model. Provide additional value, such as in-depth tutorials, access to a community, or early access to content.

Utilize crowdfunding platforms like Patreon or Ko-fi to allow your audience to support your work on a recurring basis. Provide unique perks or rewards to incentivize subscriptions.

Explore multiple monetization strategies simultaneously to minimize reliance on a single source of income. Experiment with different approaches to find the ones that work best for your audience and niche.

Seek partnerships with other content creators or businesses in your industry. Collaborate on joint projects, cross-promotions, or sponsored content to expand your reach and tap into new audiences.

Cultivate a strong relationship with your audience through consistent interaction, responding to comments, and hosting live Q&A sessions. Nurture a sense of community to foster loyalty and word-of-mouth growth.

Regularly analyze your website traffic, social media engagement, and conversion metrics. Use tools like Google Analytics, social media analytics, and sales tracking to identify patterns and trends. Optimize your content, marketing strategies, and monetization techniques based on these insights.

Utilize various social media platforms to expand your reach and attract new followers. Engage with your audience through consistent posting, responding to comments, and participating in relevant discussions.

Collaborate with brands for sponsored social media posts or influencer campaigns. Ensure that partnerships align with your brand and provide value to your audience.

Take advantage of social commerce features offered by platforms like Instagram, Facebook, or Pinterest. Utilize buy buttons, product tagging, or shoppable posts to facilitate direct sales from your social media presence.

Comply with legal regulations regarding disclosure of sponsorships, affiliate relationships, and any potential conflicts of interest. Maintain transparency with your audience to uphold trust and credibility.

Familiarize yourself with privacy regulations like the General Data Protection Regulation (GDPR) and ensure that you handle user data responsibly. Safeguard the personal information of your audience and adhere to best practices in data protection.

Respect copyright laws and intellectual property rights when using content, images, or music in your online presence. Obtain proper permissions or licenses and attribute sources appropriately.

Monetizing your online presence requires a combination of strategic planning, consistent effort, and understanding your audience's needs. By building a strong brand, employing diverse monetization strategies, and fostering a loyal community, you can transform your online presence into a profitable venture. Remember to adapt and evolve as the digital landscape changes, always prioritizing authenticity, quality, and ethical practices. Embrace the opportunities that the internet provides and unlock the full potential of your online presence.

Conduct thorough keyword research to identify the topics and search terms that are relevant to your niche. Optimize your content to rank higher in search engine results, driving organic traffic to your website or platform.

Implement on-page and technical SEO techniques, including optimizing meta tags, headers, and URLs, improving site speed, and ensuring mobile responsiveness. This will enhance your visibility and increase the likelihood of attracting organic traffic.

Collaborate with other reputable websites or blogs in your industry to contribute guest posts. In return, you can include backlinks to your own content, which can boost your website's authority and search engine rankings.

Leverage your knowledge and expertise in your niche to create comprehensive online courses. Identify the specific skills or information that your audience is seeking and structure your courses accordingly.

Utilize online learning platforms such as Udemy, Coursera, or Teachable to host and sell your courses. These platforms provide user-friendly interfaces for course creation, marketing, and payment processing.

Develop a robust marketing strategy to promote your courses. Leverage your existing online presence, engage with your audience, and create compelling sales pages or promotional videos to attract potential students.

Organize live webinars or workshops where you can share valuable insights, provide demonstrations, or offer personalized guidance to your audience. Monetize these events through ticket sales or sponsorships.

Curate virtual conferences or summits within your industry, featuring expert speakers, panel discussions, and networking opportunities. Generate revenue through ticket sales, sponsorships, or premium access options.

If you offer free content or services, consider setting up crowdfunding campaigns on platforms like Kickstarter or Patreon. Your loyal audience members can contribute financially to support your work.

Include a donation or tip jar option on your website or social media platforms. Provide value to your audience and encourage those who appreciate your work to contribute.

Continuously adapt and explore new revenue streams as technology and consumer behavior evolve. Stay informed about emerging trends, engage with your audience to understand their needs, and be willing to experiment with innovative strategies. Remember, building a profitable online presence requires persistence, creativity, and a deep understanding of your audience's preferences and desires.

Host or participate in events relevant to your niche, such as conferences, workshops, or meetups. Seek sponsorship opportunities from brands or businesses looking to reach your target audience.

Collaborate with other influential individuals or content creators in your industry. Jointly create content, host webinars, or launch co-branded products to expand your reach and tap into new markets.

Forge strategic partnerships with brands that align with your values and resonate with your audience. Negotiate sponsored content, ambassador programs, or affiliate partnerships that provide mutual benefits.

Incorporate sponsored content seamlessly within your regular content to provide value to your audience while promoting relevant products or services. Maintain transparency and clearly label sponsored posts.

Leverage video platforms like YouTube or TikTok to monetize your content through ads. Explore options like pre-roll ads, mid-roll ads, or sponsored segments to generate revenue from your video content.

Join ad revenue sharing programs, such as YouTube's Partner Program or Twitch's Affiliate Program, to earn a portion of the advertising revenue generated by the platforms.

Consider setting up a dropshipping business where you sell products without maintaining inventory. Partner with suppliers who handle inventory and shipping, allowing you to focus on marketing and sales.

Create and sell custom-designed merchandise, such as t-shirts, mugs, or phone cases, using print-on-demand services. This allows you to offer branded products without the need for inventory management.

Explore opportunities to license your brand or intellectual property for use in merchandise, collaborations, or endorsements. Partner with companies that can manufacture and distribute licensed products.

Leverage your audience and online presence to conduct surveys, gather insights, or facilitate market research for businesses. Monetize this data by providing valuable reports, analysis, or consulting services.

Build an email list and leverage it as a valuable asset. Use email marketing campaigns, lead generation forms, or sponsored newsletters to generate revenue by promoting relevant products or services to your subscribers.

Explore programmatic advertising platforms that allow you to monetize your website or platform's data by serving targeted advertisements to your audience based on their interests and behavior.

Remember, generating revenue from your online presence requires continuous effort, adaptability, and staying ahead of industry trends. Experiment with different strategies, analyze your results, and optimize your approach based on the preferences and behavior of your audience. Embrace the evolving digital landscape, be open to collaborations, and always prioritize delivering value to your audience.

Niche Selection

There's a great, big world out there – a world filled with many other dreamers and visionaries and entrepreneurs just like you wanting to find their place. Still, however, there's a place just for you. That is, if you know how to find it.

In the vast and ever-expanding realm of the internet, finding your niche is like discovering a secret treasure trove. The digital landscape offers endless opportunities for entrepreneurs and content creators to carve out their profitable corner and connect with a targeted audience. However, the process of niche selection requires careful consideration and research to ensure long-term success. In this chapter, we will explore the art of finding your profitable niche, examining strategies and insights to guide you on your journey.

Before diving into the process, let's understand what a niche truly represents. A niche is a specialized segment of a broader market, focusing on a specific interest, passion, or problem. It allows you to narrow your focus and cater to a specific audience, setting yourself apart from more general competitors.

Selecting a niche has several advantages. It enables you to establish yourself as an authority within a specific domain, enhances your chances of success by targeting a dedicated audience, and helps build a strong brand identity. Moreover, a well-defined niche allows for effective marketing, content creation, and monetization strategies.

Begin by introspecting and identifying your passions, interests, and areas of expertise. What topics do you find yourself constantly researching or discussing with others? What are your hobbies, skills, or professional experiences? By aligning your niche with your passions, you'll find greater fulfillment and motivation in your online endeavors.

Once you have identified potential niches based on your interests, conduct thorough market research. Analyze existing competition, target audience demographics, search volume, and market trends. Look for underserved areas or gaps in the market that you could fill with your unique perspective or offering.

After narrowing down your options, it's crucial to validate your chosen niche with your target audience. Engage in conversations, conduct surveys, and seek feedback from online communities or social media groups related to your niche. Pay attention to their pain points, needs, and desires. This validation process will help ensure that there is genuine demand and interest in your chosen niche.

While competition is healthy, excessive competition can make it challenging to stand out. Analyze your potential competitors within the niche. Evaluate their strategies, content quality, audience engagement, and monetization methods. Identify areas where you can differentiate yourself and offer unique value to your audience.

Assess the potential monetization avenues within your niche. Consider options like affiliate marketing, sponsored content, advertising, product creation, online courses, membership sites, or e-commerce. Study successful businesses or content creators in similar niches to understand their revenue models and adapt them to fit your niche.

Evaluate the long-term sustainability and growth potential of your chosen niche. Is there room for expansion and diversification in the future? Will the niche remain relevant as the industry evolves? Ensure that your niche has the potential to provide consistent income and withstand market fluctuations.

Define your brand identity, including your unique value proposition, tone of voice, visual aesthetics, and brand personality. Ensure consistency across your website, social media profiles, and content. Your brand should resonate with your target audience and differentiate you from competitors.

Develop a content strategy that aligns with your niche and target audience. Create high-quality, engaging content that provides value to your audience. Identify the most effective channels to distribute your content, such as a blog, YouTube channel, podcast, or social media platforms. Consistency and relevance are key in building a loyal following within your niche.

Actively engage with your audience through comments, direct messages, and community forums. Respond to their questions, address their concerns, and foster a sense of connection and trust. Encourage feedback and incorporate it into your content and offerings, further solidifying your position as a trusted authority in your niche.

The online landscape is constantly evolving, and it's essential to stay up-to-date with the latest trends, technologies, and changes within your niche. Regularly monitor industry news, participate in relevant conferences or webinars, and adapt your strategies accordingly.

As your online presence grows, you may find opportunities to expand within your niche or explore adjacent niches. Continuously assess the needs of your audience and explore new avenues for growth while maintaining a strong foundation in your core niche.

Be open to adapting your strategies and embracing change. The internet is dynamic, and what worked yesterday may not work tomorrow. Continuously evaluate your metrics, experiment with new ideas, and be willing to pivot when necessary to stay relevant and profitable.

Finding your profitable corner of the internet through niche selection requires a combination of self-reflection, market research, validation, and a keen understanding of your target audience. By aligning your passions and expertise with an underserved market segment, you can establish yourself as a valuable resource and build a successful online presence. Remember to consistently provide high-quality content, engage with your audience, and adapt to changing circumstances. With careful planning and execution, your niche selection journey can lead you to long-term profitability and fulfillment in the vast world of the internet.

To provide a practical example of niche selection and its impact, let's dive into the story of Sarah, a client and an aspiring content creator looking to establish her online presence.

Sarah has always been passionate about sustainable living and eco-friendly practices. She possesses in-depth knowledge about zero-waste living, renewable energy, and conscious consumerism. Recognizing her passion as a potential niche, Sarah decides to explore the sustainable living space further.

Sarah conducts thorough market research to understand the current landscape of sustainable living content. She identifies various blogs, YouTube channels, and social media accounts focusing on the subject. By analyzing their content, engagement levels, and audience feedback, Sarah gains insights into what works and how she can differentiate herself.

To validate her niche, Sarah engages with online communities and sustainable living forums. She listens to their concerns, joins discussions, and provides valuable insights. This process not only confirms the genuine interest in sustainable living but also helps Sarah understand the specific pain points and needs of her target audience.

Sarah explores various monetization avenues within her niche. She discovers that sustainable living offers opportunities for affiliate marketing partnerships with eco-friendly brands, collaborations with sustainable lifestyle products, and sponsored content related to eco-friendly home improvements. Additionally, Sarah plans to create her own digital products such as e-books or online courses on sustainable living practices.

Based on her niche and target audience, Sarah carefully crafts her brand identity. She chooses a warm and earthy color palette for her website and social media profiles, reflecting the natural elements associated with sustainable living. Sarah's brand voice exudes positivity, encouragement, and practical advice, fostering a sense of community and empowering her audience to make sustainable choices.

Sarah develops a content strategy that aligns with her niche and resonates with her audience. She creates informative blog posts, engaging videos showcasing sustainable lifestyle tips, and practical guides to help her audience adopt eco-friendly practices. By addressing the specific pain points and providing actionable solutions, Sarah establishes herself as a trusted authority in the sustainable living space.

To foster engagement, Sarah actively responds to comments on her blog and social media platforms. She conducts live Q&A sessions, encourages her audience to share their experiences, and features their success stories on her channels. This level of interaction strengthens the community around her niche and enhances her credibility as an expert.

Sarah stays updated on the latest sustainable living trends, such as new zero-waste products, innovative recycling methods, or emerging renewable energy technologies. She regularly attends sustainability conferences and collaborates with industry experts to provide her audience with up-to-date information and insights.

As Sarah's online presence grows, she identifies opportunities to expand her niche. She starts exploring related areas such as sustainable fashion, eco-travel, and ethical investing, broadening her content offerings while maintaining her core focus on sustainable living.

Sarah's journey exemplifies the process of niche selection and the steps required to establish a profitable online presence. By aligning her passion, expertise, and market research, Sarah successfully identified a niche within the sustainable living space. Through consistent content creation, engagement with her audience, and continuous adaptation, she built a thriving brand and a loyal community.

Remember, finding your profitable corner of the internet requires diligent research, validation, and a deep understanding of your audience. By selecting a niche that aligns with your passions, expertise, and market demand, you can create a sustainable and fulfilling online venture that stands out in the vast digital landscape.

Choose a niche that genuinely resonates with you. Authenticity and passion are key drivers of success in the online world. Your enthusiasm and genuine interest will shine through your content, establishing a deeper connection with your audience.

While competition within a niche can indicate demand, excessive competition can make it challenging to stand out. Analyze competitors' strategies, content quality, and audience engagement. Look for ways to differentiate yourself by offering a unique perspective, specialized knowledge, or a distinct voice.

When selecting a niche, consider its long-term viability. Is it a passing trend or something that will remain relevant for years to come? Look for niches with enduring appeal or those related to evergreen topics that will continue to attract interest over time.

Niche selection is about catering to a specific audience segment. Identify a target audience with a clear set of interests, problems, or aspirations. This focused approach allows you to tailor your content, products, and marketing efforts to meet their specific needs effectively.

Sometimes, niches within niches can offer untapped opportunities. Consider drilling down further into your chosen niche to discover sub-niches or specialized segments that may have less competition but still possess a dedicated audience.

Validate your niche by seeking feedback from your target audience. Engage in conversations, conduct surveys, or create a minimum viable product to test the market response. Use this feedback to refine your niche and adapt your approach accordingly.

While it's essential to follow your passion, don't overlook the profitability aspect. Conduct thorough market research to ensure that there is a viable market for your chosen niche. Look for monetization opportunities and revenue streams that align with your niche to ensure a sustainable business model.

The digital landscape is ever-evolving, and niches can change or evolve over time. Be open to adapting your niche strategy based on emerging trends, audience feedback, or shifting market dynamics. Flexibility and the ability to pivot will contribute to your long-term success.

Identify your unique strengths, experiences, or expertise that you can bring to your niche. Highlight these differentiators in your content and branding to position yourself as an authority and establish a competitive edge.

Building a profitable online presence takes time and effort. Stay committed to consistently creating valuable content, engaging with your audience, and refining your strategies. Success in niche selection comes with perseverance, dedication, and a willingness to learn and adapt.

Niche selection is a pivotal step in establishing your profitable corner of the internet. By aligning your passions, expertise, and market demand, you can carve out a space where you can thrive. Remember to conduct thorough research, validate your ideas, and remain adaptable as you navigate the dynamic online landscape. With careful niche selection, you can build a successful online venture that not only generates profits but also allows you to make a meaningful impact within your chosen niche.

Building a Solid Foundation

Congratulations on embarking on your journey to build your online business! In this chapter, we will discuss the importance of establishing a solid foundation for your venture. Just like a house needs a strong foundation to withstand the test of time, your online business requires a robust structure to ensure its longevity and success. By focusing on key areas such as planning, branding, customer experience, and scalability, you can build a strong foundation that will support your business as it grows and evolves.

Before diving into the nitty-gritty details, take a step back to define your vision and strategy. Ask yourself essential questions: What do you aim to achieve with your online business? What are your long-term goals? By clearly articulating your vision and aligning it with a strategic plan, you'll be able to make informed decisions and keep your focus in the right direction.

Understanding your target audience is crucial for any business, and it's no different for an online venture. Conduct thorough market research to identify your ideal customers. Gain insights into their needs, preferences, and pain points. This knowledge will guide your marketing efforts, allowing you to tailor your products or services to meet their expectations effectively.

Branding plays a significant role in setting your online business apart from the competition. Create a strong brand identity that reflects your values, mission, and unique selling proposition. Design a compelling logo, choose a color palette that resonates with your target audience, and develop a consistent tone of voice for your content. A strong brand presence builds trust, credibility, and customer loyalty.

Your website is the face of your online business. Ensure it provides a seamless and user-friendly experience. Optimize your site's loading speed, make it mobile-responsive, and have intuitive navigation. Include high-quality visuals and compelling copy to engage your visitors. Implement secure payment gateways and privacy policies to protect your customers' data. A well-designed website enhances your credibility and encourages conversions.

Exceptional customer experience is a cornerstone of a successful online business. Respond promptly to inquiries and provide excellent customer support. Personalize interactions whenever possible and gather feedback to continually improve your products or services. Happy customers are more likely to become repeat buyers and advocates for your brand.

No matter how remarkable your products or services are, they won't sell themselves without effective marketing. Develop a comprehensive marketing strategy that utilizes various channels such as social media, content marketing, search engine optimization, and paid advertising. Consistently monitor and analyze your marketing efforts to optimize your campaigns and maximize your return on investment.

To accommodate growth and expansion, you need a scalable infrastructure for your online business. Consider using cloud-based solutions, customer relationship management (CRM) tools, and scalable hosting services. Automate repetitive tasks where possible to increase efficiency and free up time for more strategic activities. A scalable infrastructure allows you to adapt to changing demands and seize new opportunities.

The digital landscape is constantly evolving, and staying agile is vital. Keep an eye on industry trends and emerging technologies that could impact your online business. Continuously evaluate and refine your strategies, products, and processes to remain competitive. Embrace innovation and be willing to adapt your business model as necessary.

Building a strong foundation for your online business is the bedrock of its success. By defining your vision, understanding your target audience, developing a strong brand, focusing on user experience, investing in marketing, and building a scalable infrastructure, you set your business up for long-term growth and profitability.

Communication is key in any business, especially in the online realm where direct face-to-face interactions are limited. Set up efficient communication channels to connect with your customers, partners, and employees. Utilize email marketing, social media messaging, live chat, and even chatbots to provide timely responses and address inquiries. Clear and consistent communication fosters trust and strengthens relationships.

To make informed decisions and track your progress, it's essential to monitor and analyze key metrics related to your online business. Keep a close eye on indicators such as website traffic, conversion rates, customer acquisition costs, customer lifetime value, and social media engagement. Leverage analytics tools to gain insights into your business performance and identify areas for improvement.

Collaborating with other businesses or influencers in your industry can be immensely beneficial. Seek out strategic partnerships that align with your values and target audience. Partnering with complementary brands or influential individuals can help expand your reach, increase brand exposure, and tap into new customer segments. Joint marketing campaigns, affiliate programs, or co-creating content can be mutually advantageous.

Even in the online world, fostering a strong company culture is crucial. Clearly define your company's core values and ensure they are reflected in your interactions with customers, employees, and partners. Encourage teamwork, open communication, and a positive work environment. A strong company culture not only attracts and retains talented employees but also helps create a unified brand identity and delivers consistent customer experiences.

Operating an online business comes with legal and regulatory obligations that vary across jurisdictions. Ensure you understand and comply with relevant laws and regulations pertaining to data protection, online transactions, privacy policies, and any industry-specific requirements. Staying compliant not only protects your business from legal repercussions but also builds trust with your customers.

The digital landscape is ever-evolving, and standing still is not an option. Encourage a culture of innovation within your business, fostering creativity and embracing new ideas. Stay informed about emerging technologies, market trends, and consumer preferences. Be proactive in adapting your strategies and offerings to meet evolving customer needs. By continuously innovating, you can stay ahead of the competition and seize new opportunities.

Building strong, long-term relationships with your customers is essential for sustained success. Implement strategies to nurture customer loyalty and encourage repeat business. Offer personalized experiences, loyalty programs, exclusive discounts, and valuable content.

Actively seek and incorporate customer feedback to enhance your products and services. Happy, loyal customers not only generate repeat sales but also become advocates who refer new customers to your business.

Building a strong foundation for your online business is a continuous process that requires dedication, adaptability, and strategic thinking. By focusing on key areas such as vision and strategy, branding, customer experience, scalability, communication, metrics, partnerships, company culture, compliance, innovation, and customer relationships, you can establish a solid framework that will support the growth and success of your online business for years to come. Embrace the journey, learn from challenges, and always strive for excellence in every aspect of your business.

Every successful business starts with a strong foundation. Just as a sturdy building relies on a solid base to support its structure, a thriving business needs a strong foundation to sustain growth, withstand challenges, and achieve long-term success. In this chapter, we will explore the importance of building a solid foundation for your business and how it sets the stage for future growth, profitability, and sustainability.

A strong foundation begins with a clear vision and mission for your business. Your vision defines the direction and purpose of your company, while your mission outlines the specific goals and values that guide your actions. A well-defined vision and mission statement provide clarity and focus, serving as a compass to steer your business towards success.

Building a strong foundation requires strategic planning. A comprehensive business plan helps you outline your goals, strategies, target market, and competitive landscape. It enables you to anticipate challenges, identify opportunities, and make informed decisions. A well-thought-out plan provides a roadmap for your business's growth and helps you stay on track even during uncertain times.

Understanding your target market and industry is crucial for building a strong foundation. Conduct thorough market research to identify your ideal customers, their needs, and preferences. Analyze market trends, competition, and consumer behavior to gain insights that will inform your product development, marketing strategies, and customer acquisition efforts. Solid market research lays the groundwork for effective targeting and positioning in the marketplace.

A strong brand identity sets your business apart from competitors and establishes an emotional connection with your target audience. Define your brand values, personality, and positioning. Develop a compelling brand story and visual elements that resonate with your customers.

Consistency in brand messaging across all channels builds recognition, trust, and loyalty, creating a strong foundation for long-term success.

Efficiency and effective processes are essential for a strong business foundation. Streamline your operations, workflows, and supply chain to minimize costs, reduce errors, and enhance productivity. Implement robust systems and technologies to automate repetitive tasks, track key metrics, and streamline communication. Operational efficiency creates a solid foundation for scalability and growth.

Sound financial management is vital for building a strong business foundation. Develop a realistic budget, track cash flow, and monitor key financial metrics. Implement accounting systems and processes that ensure accuracy and transparency. Maintain a healthy balance between revenue generation and expenses, and create contingency plans for unforeseen circumstances. Strong financial management provides stability and ensures your business's ability to weather economic fluctuations.

Putting the customer at the center of your business is essential for success. Prioritize customer satisfaction, understanding their needs, and delivering exceptional experiences. Build strong relationships with your customers through personalized interactions, excellent customer service, and continuous improvement based on their feedback. A customer-centric approach builds loyalty, generates positive word-of-mouth, and establishes a solid foundation for sustained growth.

Your team is a fundamental part of your business foundation. Surround yourself with talented individuals who share your vision and values. Foster a positive work culture that promotes collaboration, innovation, and growth. Invest in employee training and development to enhance their skills and expertise. A strong team aligned with your business goals provides the support and motivation needed to build a successful foundation.

The business landscape is ever-changing, and adaptability is crucial for a strong foundation. Be prepared to embrace change, pivot when necessary, and take calculated risks. Develop resilience to navigate challenges and setbacks, learning from them and incorporating those lessons into your business strategies. An adaptable and resilient business foundation ensures the ability to thrive in a dynamic marketplace.

Building a strong foundation is essential for the long-term success and sustainability of your business. By focusing on clear vision and mission, strategic planning, market research, strong brand identity, operational efficiency, financial management, customer focus, team building, and adaptability, you establish a solid base upon which your business can thrive.

A strong foundation provides stability and direction, guiding your decision-making and actions. It allows you to anticipate and navigate challenges, seize opportunities, and adapt to changing market dynamics. It instills confidence in stakeholders, including customers, investors, and employees, and sets the stage for growth and expansion.

Remember, building a strong foundation is an ongoing process. It requires continuous monitoring, evaluation, and adjustment to stay aligned with market trends and evolving customer needs. Regularly reassess your business strategies, evaluate your performance against key metrics, and stay agile in your approach.

With a strong foundation in place, you'll be well-positioned to build upon your success, expand your offerings, and reach new heights. As your business grows, the foundation you've established will provide a solid framework to support your operations, maintain your brand reputation, and foster sustainable growth.

In conclusion, invest the time and effort to build a strong foundation for your business. It is the bedrock upon which your success will be built. By focusing on the key elements outlined in this chapter, you'll be well-equipped to create a resilient, adaptable, and prosperous business that can withstand the challenges and seize the opportunities that come your way.

Leveraging Social Media

In the early years of the 21st century, a transformative phenomenon began to unfold, forever altering the way we communicate, share information, and connect with one another. Social media platforms emerged as powerful tools that would shape our society in profound and unexpected ways. This chapter delves into the rise of social media, exploring its origins, its impact on individuals and communities, and the challenges and opportunities it presents.

Social media traces its roots back to the early days of the internet when online communities and forums provided spaces for individuals to connect and exchange ideas. Platforms like Friendster and MySpace emerged in the early

2000s, marking the beginning of a new era of online interaction. These platforms introduced features such as profile pages, messaging, and the ability to share photos and interests, setting the stage for what was to come.

In 2004, Harvard University student Mark Zuckerberg launched a platform called Facebook, initially limited to college campuses. Its meteoric rise in popularity demonstrated the power of social networking. Facebook soon expanded to include users from around the world, becoming a ubiquitous presence in people's lives. The introduction of the news feed feature in 2006, enabling users to see real-time updates from their friends, fueled the platform's growth and cemented its place as a dominant force in the social media landscape.

In 2006, Twitter introduced a new concept to social media: microblogging. Users could now share their thoughts, news, and observations in short, 140-character messages known as tweets. This format revolutionized the way information spread, allowing real-time updates on events, opinions, and trending topics. Twitter became a vital tool for breaking news, activism, and public discourse, providing a platform for voices that had previously gone unheard.

The rise of visual content on social media brought about the emergence of platforms like Instagram and Snapchat. Instagram, launched in 2010, focused on sharing photos and videos, accompanied by captions and hashtags. Its user-friendly interface and emphasis on visual storytelling quickly attracted a massive following, eventually leading to its acquisition by Facebook. Snapchat, on the other hand, introduced disappearing messages and "stories," providing a more ephemeral and authentic way of sharing moments with friends.

The proliferation of social media platforms had far-reaching consequences for individuals and communities worldwide. On the positive side, it brought people closer, transcending geographical barriers and fostering connections between individuals of diverse backgrounds. It provided a platform for expression, allowing users to share their passions, creativity, and ideas. Social media played a pivotal role in mobilizing social and political movements, enabling grassroots activism and raising awareness about various issues.

However, the rise of social media also presented challenges. Privacy concerns emerged as users grappled with the implications of sharing personal information online. The addictive nature of social media, characterized by endless scrolling and curated feeds, raised concerns about mental health and its impact on well-being. The spread of misinformation and the echo chamber effect, where individuals are only exposed to like-minded views, posed threats to democracy and societal cohesion.

Social media continues to evolve rapidly, adapting to changing user preferences and technological advancements. New platforms emerge, each with its unique features and target audience. TikTok, for instance, gained immense popularity among younger users with its short-form videos and creative editing tools. LinkedIn established itself as the go-to platform for professional networking, while platforms like Twitch and YouTube catered to the growing demand for live streaming and content creation.

The rise of social media transformed the way we connect, communicate, and interact with one another in the digital age. It has become an integral part of our daily lives, influencing our relationships, our access to information, and our understanding of the world. As social media platforms continue to evolve and shape our society, it is crucial to recognize both the opportunities and challenges they present.

One of the significant opportunities of social media lies in its ability to amplify marginalized voices and foster inclusivity. Previously unheard individuals and communities now have a platform to share their stories, experiences, and perspectives, challenging existing power structures and bringing attention to social injustices. Movements like #BlackLivesMatter and #MeToo gained momentum through social media, sparking important conversations and driving real-world change.

Additionally, social media has transformed the way businesses and brands interact with consumers. It offers unprecedented opportunities for marketing, advertising, and customer engagement. Influencer culture has emerged, where individuals with large social media followings can effectively shape consumer behavior and influence purchasing decisions. Social media platforms have become virtual marketplaces, enabling entrepreneurs and small businesses to reach global audiences and thrive in the digital economy.

However, the rise of social media also presents significant challenges that must be addressed. The spread of fake news, misinformation, and disinformation has become a pressing issue, undermining public trust and distorting our collective understanding of reality. Algorithms that prioritize engagement and user retention can create echo chambers, reinforcing biases and limiting exposure to diverse perspectives. The impact of social media on mental health is a growing concern, as excessive use, cyberbullying, and the constant comparison to idealized online personas contribute to anxiety, depression, and other psychological issues.

To mitigate these challenges, individuals, communities, and platforms themselves must take responsibility. Digital literacy education is crucial to equip users with the skills to navigate the online world critically. Platforms must prioritize transparency, algorithmic accountability, and user privacy. Regulatory frameworks should be developed to address issues of data protection, content moderation, and the ethical use of user data. Users themselves should practice mindful and responsible engagement, being aware of the potential pitfalls of social media while leveraging its benefits.

As we look to the future, the trajectory of social media remains uncertain. Technological advancements like virtual reality, augmented reality, and artificial intelligence are likely to shape the next generation of social media platforms. These advancements will offer new possibilities for connection, communication, and expression. However, as we embrace these innovations, we must also reflect on the impact they have on our lives, relationships, and societies. By fostering a culture of digital citizenship, responsible usage, and collective accountability, we can harness the power of social media for the greater good while mitigating its potential drawbacks.

The rise of social media has been a transformative force, reshaping the way we connect, share, and engage with the world. Its impact on society is profound, offering new avenues for expression, mobilization, and economic opportunities. Yet, it is crucial that we navigate the challenges it presents with foresight and responsibility, ensuring that social media remains a tool for empowerment, understanding, and positive change in our increasingly interconnected global community.

In today's digital landscape, social media platforms have become powerful tools for entrepreneurs and business owners to establish and grow their online ventures. This chapter explores the strategies, best practices, and considerations for leveraging social media to build a profitable online business. From creating a strong brand presence to engaging with your target audience, we will delve into the key steps you need to take to maximize the potential of social media for your business.

Before diving into social media, it is crucial to define your brand identity and identify your target audience. Clearly articulate your business's mission, values, and unique selling proposition. Determine the demographics, interests, and preferences of your target audience to tailor your social media efforts effectively. This foundational work will guide your content creation, engagement strategies, and overall branding on social media.

With an abundance of social media platforms available, it's important to choose the ones that align with your business goals and target audience. Conduct research to understand which platforms your target audience frequents the most and where your industry's influencers and competitors have a strong presence. Consider platforms such as Facebook, Instagram, LinkedIn, Twitter, and YouTube, among others. Each platform offers unique features and user demographics, allowing you to tailor your approach accordingly.

Content is the lifeblood of any successful social media strategy. Develop a content plan that aligns with your brand's voice and resonates with your target audience. Create a mix of engaging and valuable content, such as informative articles, captivating visuals, videos, infographics, and user-generated content. Strive to provide educational, entertaining, or inspirational content that addresses your audience's pain points and encourages them to engage with your brand.

Social media is not just about broadcasting your message; it's about fostering meaningful connections and building a community around your brand. Engage with your audience by responding to comments, messages, and mentions promptly. Encourage user-generated content and facilitate conversations through contests, polls, and discussions. Collaborate with influencers, industry experts, and like-minded businesses to extend your reach and credibility. By cultivating a loyal and engaged community, you can increase brand advocacy and drive customer loyalty.

Social media advertising and promotions can significantly enhance your business's visibility and reach. Each platform provides various advertising options, including targeted ads, sponsored posts, and influencer partnerships. Develop a comprehensive advertising strategy that aligns with your goals and budget. Conduct thorough audience targeting, use compelling visuals, and craft persuasive ad copy to maximize your return on investment.

To ensure the effectiveness of your social media efforts, continuously analyze and adjust your strategies based on data and insights. Utilize social media analytics tools to track key metrics such as reach, engagement, click-through rates, and conversions. Identify the content and strategies that resonate most with your audience and optimize your approach accordingly. Regularly evaluate the performance of your campaigns, test new ideas, and refine your social media strategy to achieve optimal results.

Social media landscape is ever-evolving, with new trends and technologies emerging regularly.

Stay informed and embrace relevant trends to keep your online business at the forefront. Stay up-to-date with platform updates, algorithm changes, and new features. Explore emerging technologies like live video streaming, augmented reality filters, or chatbots, which can enhance customer experiences and differentiate your brand from competitors.

Social media has revolutionized the way businesses establish and grow their online presence. By leveraging the power of social media platforms, entrepreneurs can reach a vast audience, engage with customers, and drive profitability for their online businesses. However, success on social media requires a strategic and thoughtful approach.

It's important to remember that building a profitable online business through social media takes time and effort. Consistency is key - regularly post valuable content, engage with your audience, and monitor the performance of your efforts. It's also essential to adapt to changes in the social media landscape, as platforms evolve, algorithms change, and user behaviors shift.

Be genuine in your interactions and portray your brand's authentic voice. Transparency builds trust with your audience and fosters a sense of credibility. Share behind-the-scenes glimpses, highlight your team, and showcase the values that drive your business. Authenticity goes a long way in establishing a strong connection with your audience.

Influencer marketing can be a valuable strategy for expanding your reach and gaining credibility. Identify influencers in your niche or industry who align with your brand values and have an engaged following. Collaborate with them on sponsored posts, product reviews, or partnerships to tap into their audience and benefit from their influence.

Social media provides a direct channel for customers to provide feedback, ask questions, and voice concerns. Actively monitor comments, messages, and reviews, and respond promptly and thoughtfully. By addressing customer feedback, you demonstrate your commitment to customer satisfaction and improve brand perception.

Reward your social media followers with exclusive promotions, discounts, or early access to new products or services. This fosters a sense of loyalty and encourages engagement. Use social media to run contests, giveaways, or limited-time offers to create a sense of urgency and excitement around your brand.

Identify complementary businesses in your industry or niche and explore collaboration opportunities. This could include cross-promotion, joint campaigns, or even co-creating products or services. By leveraging each other's audiences and expertise, you can expand your reach and tap into new customer segments.

While organic reach and engagement are valuable, social media advertising can significantly boost your visibility and reach. Allocate a portion of your marketing budget to targeted ads, retargeting campaigns, and sponsored content. Test different ad formats, audiences, and messaging to optimize your ad performance and drive conversions.

The social media landscape is constantly evolving, with new features, platforms, and trends emerging regularly. Stay updated on the latest industry news and developments. Attend webinars, conferences, or workshops, and join relevant communities or forums to learn from peers and industry experts. Embrace a growth mindset and be willing to adapt your strategies based on new insights and trends.

Social media offers immense opportunities for entrepreneurs to establish and grow their online businesses profitably. By defining your brand, creating compelling content, engaging with your audience, and utilizing advertising effectively, you can leverage social media to drive awareness, engagement, and conversions. Stay adaptable, monitor your performance, and continuously refine your strategies to stay ahead in the ever-changing social media landscape.

Make sure your social media profiles are complete, visually appealing, and optimized for search. Use relevant keywords in your bio, include a link to your website or online store, and use high-quality images that represent your brand. A well-optimized profile increases your chances of being discovered by potential customers and improves your credibility.

Take advantage of the analytics tools provided by social media platforms. Analyze key metrics such as reach, engagement, click-through rates, and conversions. Understand which types of content perform best, what times your audience is most active, and which platforms drive the most traffic and sales. Use these insights to refine your content strategy and make data-driven decisions.

If you have an online store, explore e-commerce features available on social media platforms. Many platforms, such as Facebook and Instagram, offer integrated shopping functionalities, allowing users to purchase products directly from their feeds. Enable these features to streamline the buying process and improve conversion rates.

In addition to collaborating with established influencers, consider working with micro-influencers who have a smaller but highly engaged following. Micro-influencers often have a more niche audience and can provide more targeted exposure for your brand. Their recommendations and endorsements carry significant weight with their loyal followers, making them valuable partners for your online business.

Encourage your customers and followers to create and share content related to your brand. User-generated content not only helps build trust and authenticity but also provides valuable social proof. Repost and highlight UGC on your social media channels, giving credit to the creators. This not only engages your audience but also acts as free promotion for your business.

Social media has become a customer service channel, so prioritize responsiveness and provide excellent support to your customers. Respond promptly to inquiries, address concerns, and resolve issues in a professional and courteous manner. By delivering exceptional customer service, you build a positive reputation, foster customer loyalty, and encourage positive word-of-mouth recommendations.

Stay informed about the latest trends, news, and developments in your industry. Monitor relevant hashtags, join industry-specific groups or communities, and engage in conversations. By actively participating in industry discussions and adapting your content and offerings to align with emerging trends, you position your business as a knowledgeable and forward-thinking brand.

Identify influential publications, blogs, or online magazines in your industry and establish partnerships with them. Contribute guest articles, offer product samples for review, or collaborate on sponsored content. Partnering with reputable and authoritative sources can significantly enhance your brand's visibility, credibility, and reach.

Remember, social media success is not solely measured by the number of followers, but by the engagement, conversions, and profitability it generates for your online business. Continuously experiment, learn from your audience's feedback, and adapt your strategies accordingly. With a thoughtful and strategic approach, social media can become a powerful tool for driving profitability and long-term success for your online business.

The Power of Content Marketing

In today's rapidly evolving world, the internet has become an integral part of our daily lives. It has revolutionized the way we communicate, gather information, and conduct business. One of the most remarkable aspects of the internet is its ability to provide countless opportunities for individuals to generate income. In this chapter, we will explore the importance of generating income online and how it can positively impact your financial well-being.

One of the significant advantages of generating income online is the freedom and flexibility it offers. Unlike traditional jobs, online income streams allow you to work from anywhere, be it the comfort of your home, a bustling coffee shop, or even while traveling. This flexibility enables you to create a work-life balance that suits your needs and allows you to pursue other interests or spend quality time with loved ones.

The online world knows no boundaries when it comes to potential income generation. Unlike traditional jobs that often have fixed salaries, online ventures have unlimited earning potential. Whether you choose to sell products, provide services, create content, or engage in affiliate marketing, the internet provides a global marketplace where you can reach a vast audience and tap into diverse revenue streams. With determination, creativity, and strategic thinking, the sky's the limit in terms of what you can achieve financially.

Starting a traditional brick-and-mortar business can be financially challenging, with significant upfront costs. However, generating income online often requires minimal investment. Many online platforms and marketplaces provide a low-cost or even free entry point for individuals to start their ventures. Whether it's setting up an online store, creating a blog, or offering freelance services, you can start with little to no capital and gradually scale up your operations as you generate income.

The online world offers a plethora of income-generating opportunities, allowing you to diversify your revenue streams. By exploring different online ventures simultaneously, you can reduce the risks associated with relying solely on a single income source. For instance, you could combine selling products on an e-commerce platform with earning advertising revenue from a blog or YouTube channel. This diversification not only safeguards you against potential setbacks but also increases the potential for passive income, where you earn money even while you're not actively working.

Engaging in online income generation opens up a world of learning and personal growth. Whether it's mastering new skills, understanding digital marketing strategies, or honing your creativity, the online realm offers endless opportunities for self-improvement. Additionally, you'll gain insights into the ever-evolving digital landscape, equipping you with valuable knowledge that can be applied to various aspects of life, including future job prospects, entrepreneurship, and adapting to technological advancements.

The world of work is rapidly changing, and the COVID-19 pandemic has highlighted the importance of adaptability and resilience. Generating income online equips you with valuable digital skills that can help you thrive in the face of uncertainty. With the ability to pivot quickly, leverage emerging trends, and tap into various online platforms, you'll be better equipped to navigate the challenges that arise in the evolving job market.

Generating income online has become increasingly essential in our interconnected world. It provides unparalleled freedom, flexibility, and financial potential, all while offering low start-up costs, diversification, and opportunities for personal growth. Embracing the online realm can empower you to take control of your financial future, opening doors to a world of possibilities and paving the way for a prosperous and fulfilling life. So, seize the opportunities presented by the digital age and embark on your online income-generating journey today!

In the digital age, content marketing has emerged as a powerful strategy for businesses to connect with their target audience, build brand awareness, and drive conversions. In this chapter, we will delve into the intricacies of content marketing and how it works in the context of online businesses.

Content marketing is a strategic approach that involves creating and distributing valuable, relevant, and consistent content to attract and engage a specific target audience. The content can take various forms, such as blog posts, articles, videos, infographics, podcasts, and social media posts. The primary objective is to provide valuable information, entertain, inspire, or educate the audience while subtly promoting the brand or its products and services.

Content marketing is an effective tool for online businesses to build brand awareness. By consistently creating high-quality and valuable content, businesses can establish themselves as thought leaders, industry experts, and trusted sources of information. This helps to cultivate a loyal following and create a positive brand perception in the minds of the target audience. As a result, when potential customers are ready to make a purchase, they are more likely to choose a brand they recognize and trust.

A crucial aspect of content marketing is understanding and targeting the right audience. Online businesses must conduct thorough market research to identify their target demographic's preferences, needs, and pain points. This knowledge enables businesses to create content that resonates with their audience and provides solutions to their problems. By crafting content specifically tailored to their target audience, businesses can maximize engagement, increase traffic to their website, and attract potential customers who are more likely to convert.

In the online world, visibility is key, and search engine optimization (SEO) plays a vital role in content marketing. By optimizing content for relevant keywords, incorporating meta tags, and improving website structure and load times, businesses can enhance their online visibility and attract organic traffic from search engines. A well-executed SEO strategy ensures that content ranks higher in search engine results, making it more accessible to the target audience and increasing the chances of engagement and conversion.

The success of content marketing lies in creating engaging and compelling content that captivates the audience. Online businesses should focus on delivering value to their audience by providing informative, entertaining, or inspiring content. The content should be well-researched, well-written, and visually appealing, incorporating relevant images, videos, or infographics. By evoking emotions, sparking conversations, and encouraging social sharing, businesses can expand their reach, attract new customers, and foster a sense of community around their brand.

To ensure the effectiveness of content marketing efforts, online businesses need to measure and analyze the results. Various analytics tools and platforms provide insights into metrics such as website traffic, engagement rates, time spent on page, social media interactions, and conversion rates. By tracking these metrics, businesses can assess the performance of their content marketing campaigns, identify areas for improvement, and make data-driven decisions to optimize their content strategy.

Content marketing is a powerful and essential component of online businesses' success. By creating valuable, targeted, and engaging content, businesses can build brand awareness, establish themselves as industry leaders, attract organic traffic, and drive conversions. To thrive in the competitive online landscape, businesses must invest in understanding their target audience, optimizing content for search engines, and consistently delivering high-quality content. By leveraging the dynamics of content marketing, online businesses can forge meaningful connections with their audience, establish a competitive edge, and achieve long-term growth and success.

Creating high-quality content is only half the battle; effectively distributing and promoting that content is equally important. Online businesses should employ a multi-channel approach to reach their target audience. This includes sharing content on social media platforms, email marketing campaigns, guest posting on relevant websites, participating in online communities and forums, and collaborating with influencers or industry experts. By leveraging various distribution channels, businesses can expand their reach, attract new audiences, and drive traffic back to their website or landing pages.

Content marketing allows online businesses to build trust and establish authority within their niche. By consistently delivering valuable and reliable content, businesses can position themselves as experts and thought leaders. This fosters trust among the audience, which is crucial for converting them into loyal customers. Sharing case studies, testimonials, and success stories further reinforces the credibility of the business. When consumers perceive a brand as trustworthy and authoritative, they are more likely to engage, purchase, and recommend its products or services.

In today's era of personalized experiences, content marketing provides an opportunity for online businesses to deliver tailored messaging to their audience. By segmenting their target audience based on demographics, preferences, and behavior, businesses can create content that speaks directly to the specific needs and interests of each segment. Personalization helps in forging deeper connections, increasing engagement, and driving higher conversion rates. Leveraging customer data and analytics, businesses can understand their audience better and deliver content that resonates on an individual level.

The digital landscape is constantly evolving, and successful online businesses must stay agile and adapt to changing trends and technologies. Content marketing strategies need to be flexible and adaptable to capitalize on emerging platforms and audience preferences. Keeping an eye on industry developments, embracing new content formats, and leveraging emerging technologies, such as virtual reality or interactive content, can help businesses stay relevant and maintain a competitive edge. By continuously innovating and evolving, businesses can attract and retain an engaged audience in the ever-evolving online ecosystem.

Feedback plays a vital role in refining and optimizing content marketing efforts. Online businesses should actively seek feedback from their audience through comments, social media interactions, surveys, and user-generated content. This feedback helps businesses understand what resonates with their audience, identify areas for improvement, and iterate their content strategy accordingly. By consistently analyzing and incorporating feedback, businesses can enhance the quality, relevance, and effectiveness of their content, leading to better engagement and conversions.

Content marketing is a dynamic and ever-evolving practice in the online business world. By understanding their audience, creating valuable content, distributing it effectively, and adapting to changing trends, businesses can leverage the power of content to build brand awareness, establish authority, and drive conversions. Through personalization, trust-building, and continuous improvement, online businesses can forge meaningful connections with their audience, foster brand loyalty, and achieve long-term success in the digital realm. Embracing the nuances of content marketing and consistently delivering exceptional content will set businesses on the path to online growth and profitability.

An effective content marketing strategy involves repurposing and creating evergreen content. Repurposing content involves taking existing pieces of content and adapting them into different formats or mediums. For example, a blog post can be transformed into a video or a podcast episode. This approach allows businesses to reach a wider audience and extend the lifespan of their content. Evergreen content refers to timeless and enduring pieces that remain relevant regardless of the passage of time. By creating evergreen content, businesses can attract continuous traffic and engagement, as these pieces provide value to readers or viewers long after their initial publication.

Storytelling is a powerful tool in content marketing that helps businesses establish an emotional connection with their audience. Humans are naturally drawn to narratives, and by incorporating storytelling elements into their content, businesses can evoke emotions, engage readers, and create memorable experiences. Storytelling can take various forms, such as sharing personal anecdotes, customer success stories, or even fictional narratives that align with the brand's values and messaging. By tapping into the power of storytelling, businesses can differentiate themselves and forge deeper connections with their audience.

User-generated content (UGC) is content created by the audience or customers of a business.

Encouraging and leveraging UGC can be a valuable aspect of content marketing. When customers share their experiences, testimonials, or reviews, it not only provides social proof but also generates authentic and relatable content. UGC can be utilized in various ways, such as featuring customer stories on a website, sharing user-generated images on social media, or incorporating customer reviews into content. By involving the audience in content creation, businesses can enhance engagement, build trust, and strengthen their community.

Content curation involves gathering and sharing valuable content created by others within the industry or niche. By curating content that aligns with their audience's interests, businesses can position themselves as a valuable resource and authority in the field. Curated content can be shared on social media, blog posts, or newsletters, giving credit to the original creators and providing additional perspectives and insights to the audience. Collaboration with influencers, industry experts, or complementary businesses is another effective content marketing strategy. Collaborative content can help reach new audiences, tap into existing communities, and leverage the expertise and credibility of partners.

To ensure the effectiveness of content marketing efforts, businesses must continually monitor and analyze key metrics. Metrics such as website traffic, engagement rates, conversion rates, and social media analytics provide insights into the performance of content and the overall content marketing strategy. By regularly reviewing these metrics, businesses can identify trends, assess the impact of different content types, and make data-driven decisions to optimize their content marketing efforts. Adapting based on metrics allows businesses to refine their strategies, focus on what works best, and drive continuous improvement.

Content marketing plays a vital role in the success of online businesses. By repurposing content, creating evergreen pieces, storytelling, leveraging user-generated content, curating relevant content, and collaborating with others, businesses can engage their audience, build trust, and extend their reach. Monitoring and adapting to metrics ensure that content marketing efforts remain effective and impactful. With a well-crafted and strategic content marketing approach, online businesses can cultivate a loyal customer base, foster brand advocacy, and ultimately drive sustainable growth and success in the digital realm.

In the world of business, understanding your target audience is crucial for success. Regardless of how amazing your product or service may be, it's essential to find the right audience who will appreciate and benefit from what you have to offer. This chapter will delve into the significance of identifying and connecting with your audience, as well as provide practical insights on how to achieve this in your business endeavors.

Knowing your audience allows you to tailor your marketing efforts, products, and services to meet their specific needs. It ensures that you are investing your resources effectively, rather than spreading yourself too thin.

Conduct thorough market research to gain insights into your potential customers. Analyze demographics, interests, purchasing habits, and any other relevant information that can help you create accurate buyer personas.

When you know your audience, you can develop offerings that directly cater to their preferences, making them more likely to choose your business over competitors.

Crafting targeted messages that resonate with your audience's pain points, desires, and aspirations is crucial for effective communication. Speak their language and address their specific concerns to establish a strong connection.

By understanding your audience, you can choose the most suitable marketing channels to reach them effectively. This minimizes wasted efforts and maximizes your return on investment.

Tailor your marketing campaigns to match the preferences and habits of your target audience. Utilize digital tools like social media targeting, email marketing, and content marketing to engage with them directly.

When you understand your audience, you can provide a better customer experience by addressing their specific needs and pain points. This leads to increased customer satisfaction and loyalty.

Actively seek feedback from your audience to understand their evolving needs. This can be done through surveys, focus groups, social media interactions, and customer reviews. Use this feedback to improve your offerings and maintain a competitive edge.

By understanding your audience better than your competitors, you gain a significant advantage in the market. This allows you to offer unique value and stand out from the crowd.

As you build relationships with your audience, you gain valuable insights into their changing preferences and emerging trends. This positions your business to adapt and innovate, ensuring you remain relevant in a dynamic market.

In the realm of business, finding your audience is essential for long-term success. Understanding their needs, preferences, and pain points enables you to tailor your offerings, develop effective marketing strategies, build customer relationships, and stay ahead of the competition. Embrace the power of audience-centric thinking, and watch your business flourish as you connect with the people who truly appreciate and benefit from what you have to offer.

In the ever-expanding digital landscape, search engines have become the go-to resource for individuals seeking information, products, and services. As a result, businesses must understand the significance of Search Engine Optimization

(SEO) to thrive online. This chapter will delve into the meaning of SEO, its impact on online visibility and organic traffic, and provide insights into effective SEO strategies for businesses.

SEO refers to the process of optimizing a website and its content to improve its visibility and organic (non-paid) search engine rankings. It involves various techniques and strategies aimed at making a website more appealing to search engines like Google, Bing, and Yahoo.

In an era where competition for online attention is fierce, SEO allows businesses to increase their chances of being discovered by their target audience. It helps drive organic traffic to a website, leading to higher visibility, brand exposure, and potential conversions.

This aspect of SEO involves optimizing individual web pages, including elements such as keyword research, meta tags, headings, content optimization, URL structure, and internal linking. On-page SEO ensures that search engines can understand and rank the content effectively.

Off-page SEO focuses on activities outside the website that impact its search engine rankings. This includes building high-quality backlinks, social media engagement, influencer outreach, and online reputation management. Off-page SEO signals to search engines that the website is authoritative and trustworthy.

Ranking higher in search engine results pages (SERPs) through effective SEO techniques leads to increased organic traffic to a website. This targeted traffic is more likely to convert into customers, as they are actively searching for products or services related to your industry.

SEO involves optimizing various elements that enhance user experience, such as website speed, mobile-friendliness, easy navigation, and engaging content. A positive user experience not only encourages visitors to stay longer on your site but also leads to higher conversion rates.

Compared to paid advertising methods, SEO can be a cost-effective long-term strategy. While it requires an investment of time and effort, the benefits of higher organic rankings and sustained visibility can be significant over time, reducing the reliance on paid advertising.

Thorough keyword research helps identify the terms and phrases your target audience is using to search for products or services. By incorporating these keywords naturally into your website content, you increase the likelihood of ranking higher in relevant search results.

Creating high-quality, relevant, and informative content is crucial for SEO success. Optimizing your content with target keywords, using headings and subheadings, and incorporating multimedia elements helps search engines understand its relevance and value.

Building high-quality backlinks from reputable websites signals to search engines that your website is trustworthy and authoritative. Engage in ethical link-building practices such as guest blogging, influencer collaborations, and industry partnerships to strengthen your website's link profile.

Implementing tools like Google Analytics allows you to track the performance of your SEO efforts. Monitor key metrics such as organic traffic, bounce rates, conversion rates, and keyword rankings to assess the effectiveness of your strategies and make necessary adjustments.

SEO is an ever-evolving field, with search engines continually updating their algorithms. Stay informed about the latest trends, algorithm changes, and best practices through industry publications, forums, and reputable SEO blogs. Regularly update your SEO strategies to align with the current SEO landscape and maintain your website's visibility.

SEO plays a pivotal role in the online success of businesses today. By understanding the meaning of SEO and implementing effective strategies, businesses can improve their visibility in search engine results, drive organic traffic to their websites, and ultimately increase conversions. Embrace the power of SEO as a long-term investment in your online presence, and watch as your business thrives in the digital realm.

For businesses with a physical presence or targeting a specific geographic area, local SEO is crucial. Optimizing for local searches helps businesses appear in relevant local listings, map results, and local directories, enhancing visibility among local customers.

Create and optimize your Google My Business (GMB) profile to improve your local SEO. Ensure accurate and up-to-date information such as address, phone number, business hours, and customer reviews. Regularly post updates, engage with customer reviews, and leverage GMB features like Google Maps and Q&A to enhance your local presence.

With the majority of internet users accessing the web through mobile devices, having a mobile-friendly website is essential. Optimize your website for mobile devices by implementing responsive design, fast loading times, and easy navigation to provide a seamless mobile experience for users.

Consider mobile-specific SEO factors such as mobile-friendly content, mobile-focused keywords, and optimizing for voice search queries. Optimize your website's structure and content to ensure it is easily accessible and ranks well in mobile search results.

As voice-activated virtual assistants like Siri, Alexa, and Google Assistant gain popularity, optimizing for voice search queries becomes increasingly important. Focus on long-tail conversational keywords and create content that directly answers common voice search queries to capture this growing market.

Search engines increasingly prioritize user experience, and Core Web Vitals have gained significance. Elements like website loading speed, mobile responsiveness, and user-friendly navigation contribute to a positive user experience and impact SEO rankings.

Featured snippets provide concise answers to user queries directly on the search engine results page. Structured data markup helps search engines understand and present your content in a more visually appealing and informative manner, increasing the chances of appearing in featured snippets.

SEO is a dynamic and ever-evolving field, and businesses must stay abreast of the latest trends and best practices to maintain their online presence. Embrace local SEO, optimize for mobile devices, and adapt to emerging trends like voice search and user experience. By understanding the meaning of SEO and implementing effective strategies, businesses can achieve higher visibility, attract targeted organic traffic, and ultimately drive business growth in the online world. Embrace the power of SEO as a continuous effort, and watch your business flourish in the digital landscape.

In today's digital age, having a strong online presence is crucial for the success of any business. Search Engine Optimization (SEO) plays a vital role in helping businesses establish visibility, attract organic traffic, and achieve long-term growth. This chapter will delve into the importance of SEO for your online business, highlighting its impact on website visibility, brand awareness, and customer acquisition.

SEO ensures that your website appears prominently in search engine results when users search for relevant keywords or phrases related to your business. By optimizing your website, you increase its visibility and the likelihood of attracting organic search traffic.

When your website consistently appears in search results for relevant queries, it establishes your brand's authority and credibility. This, in turn, enhances brand perception and fosters trust among potential customers.

SEO allows you to target specific keywords and phrases that are relevant to your business. By optimizing your website for these keywords, you increase the chances of appearing in search results when users are actively looking for products or services like yours, thereby boosting brand visibility and awareness.

SEO can help your business reach a wider audience, both locally and globally. With effective optimization strategies, you can target specific geographic locations, languages, or demographics, ensuring that your brand message reaches the right audience.

SEO focuses on attracting organic traffic, which refers to visitors who find your website through search engine results rather than through paid advertisements. Organic traffic tends to be more valuable as these users have actively expressed an interest in your products or services.

Quality SEO drives targeted traffic to your website, increasing the chances of conversion. When your website appears in search results for relevant queries, users are more likely to visit, explore, and engage with your content, leading to higher conversion rates.

SEO provides long-term benefits and is a cost-effective marketing strategy compared to other forms of digital advertising. While it requires time, effort, and expertise, the results of effective

SEO can be sustained over time, reducing your dependence on paid advertising.

While paid advertising can deliver immediate results, it requires ongoing investment. SEO, on the other hand, focuses on improving your website's organic rankings, which can continue to drive traffic and generate leads even if you reduce or pause your advertising spend.

In a competitive online landscape, SEO gives you a competitive edge. By optimizing your website and content, you can outrank competitors in search engine results, attracting more visibility and potential customers.

Search engines frequently update their algorithms to deliver the most relevant and valuable results to users. By staying informed about these changes and adapting your SEO strategies accordingly, you can maintain and improve your rankings, staying ahead of your competitors.

SEO allows you to measure and track the performance of your website, keywords, and overall SEO efforts. Analytical tools provide valuable data on website traffic, user behavior, keyword rankings, and conversion rates, enabling you to make informed decisions and optimize your strategies for better results.

SEO is an iterative process. By analyzing the data and insights gained from SEO metrics, you can identify areas for improvement, refine your strategies, and drive continuous growth for your online business.

A well-optimized website that ranks high in search engine results signals to users that your business is trustworthy and authoritative. Users tend to trust websites that appear on the first page of search results, and SEO helps you achieve that level of visibility and credibility.

SEO focuses not only on optimizing for search engines but also on enhancing the user experience. By providing users with a seamless and user-friendly website, you build trust and encourage them to engage with your content, products, or services.

SEO is a long-term strategy that can provide sustainable growth for your online business. As you consistently optimize your website and content, you build a strong foundation that can attract organic traffic and generate leads over an extended period.

Compared to other marketing channels, SEO offers a high return on investment. As your website gains visibility, attracts targeted traffic, and converts users into customers, the ROI of your SEO efforts becomes evident in the form of increased sales and revenue.

In the competitive online landscape, SEO is no longer an option but a necessity for any business with an online presence. By understanding the importance of SEO and implementing effective strategies, you can increase your website's visibility, enhance brand awareness, attract quality traffic, and achieve long-term growth. SEO provides a cost-effective and sustainable marketing approach that builds trust, establishes credibility, and positions your business for success in the digital realm. Embrace the power of SEO and unlock the full potential of your online business.

Creating Digital Products

Wealth is continuously being moved around in each passing moment, and as a business owner and entrepreneur, it's time to begin leveraging the global asset to your advantage. In a world driven by consumerism, the act of shopping has become an integral part of our daily lives. From groceries to clothing, gadgets to automobiles, billions of people engage in transactions that power the global economy. In this chapter, we will explore the staggering magnitude of annual spending by shoppers worldwide, shedding light on the vast financial ecosystem that fuels industries and shapes our modern society.

Over the past century, the world has witnessed a consumer revolution of unprecedented scale. As incomes rose and access to goods and services expanded, people's spending habits underwent a dramatic transformation. Today, shopping extends beyond mere necessity; it has become a form of self-expression, an avenue for personal fulfillment, and even a social activity. As a result, the global economy has flourished, with businesses catering to diverse demands and creating a thriving marketplace.

Measuring the exact amount of money spent by shoppers globally is a daunting task due to the vastness and complexity of the marketplace. Nevertheless, economists, statisticians, and market research firms employ various methodologies to estimate these figures. According to the most recent data available, the annual global expenditure by shoppers is estimated to be in the trillions of dollars.

The retail sector, encompassing both brick-and-mortar stores and e-commerce, stands at the forefront of the global shopper's economy. Its influence is undeniable, as individuals worldwide engage in the purchase of goods ranging from daily essentials to luxury items. The retail industry provides employment to millions and drives economic growth by stimulating production, trade, and investment.

The rise of the internet and digital technologies has revolutionized the shopping experience, giving birth to the e-commerce boom. Online platforms and marketplaces have made shopping more accessible, convenient, and diverse. As a result, e-commerce has experienced exponential growth, capturing a significant share of the global shopper's expenditure. With the ease of ordering products from the comfort of their homes, consumers have embraced the digital revolution, shaping new paradigms of retail.

Understanding the spending patterns and demographics of shoppers is crucial to comprehending the scale and dynamics of global expenditure. Factors such as income levels, cultural preferences, age, and geographic location significantly influence consumer behavior. For instance, developed nations often exhibit higher per capita spending due to higher disposable incomes, while emerging economies contribute to the growth of the global shopper's economy as their middle class expands.

The magnitude of global spending by shoppers generates numerous impacts and consequences. On one hand, it drives economic growth, fosters innovation, and creates job opportunities, leading to improved standards of living for many. However, unchecked consumerism can also contribute to environmental degradation, resource depletion, and wealth inequality. Balancing the economic benefits of shopping with sustainable practices and conscious consumption is an ongoing challenge for individuals, businesses, and policymakers alike.

The annual expenditure by shoppers worldwide represents the economic heartbeat of our globalized society. From the local marketplaces to the vast digital realms, billions of transactions shape the fate of industries and economies. Understanding the scale and impact of this immense financial ecosystem empowers us to navigate the world of commerce more consciously and make informed choices as we contribute to the perpetual cycle of consumption.

The world of shopping is not merely a passive act of spending money; it is a powerful expression of consumer choice. Every purchase made contributes to shaping the market, influencing businesses, and driving the production of goods and services. As shoppers, we possess the ability to support ethical practices, sustainable production, and social responsibility by consciously selecting the brands and products that align with our values.

While global spending by shoppers encompasses a vast range of countries and regions, there are notable disparities in terms of expenditure levels. Developed nations often exhibit higher per capita spending due to factors like higher incomes, greater access to credit, and a wider range of available products. However, emerging markets are rapidly gaining momentum, with their growing middle class and increasing purchasing power contributing significantly to the global shopper's economy.

The sheer volume of spending by shoppers has far-reaching effects on industries across the globe. Retailers, manufacturers, and service providers constantly adapt to meet changing consumer demands, launching innovative products, and refining their marketing strategies. The competition among businesses to capture a share of the consumer's wallet fuels economic growth, fosters creativity, and drives technological advancements.

Throughout the year, various seasonal peaks and consumer events significantly impact the annual expenditure by shoppers. Festivals, holidays, and special occasions often witness a surge in spending, as individuals indulge in gift-giving, travel, and celebration. Prominent examples include Black Friday and Cyber Monday, where retailers offer enticing discounts, resulting in a frenzy of shopping activity. These events generate substantial revenue for businesses, shaping annual sales figures and financial projections.

With the rise of digital platforms, targeted advertising and personalized marketing have become prevalent strategies to capture consumer attention and drive spending. Online retailers and social media platforms leverage vast amounts of data to tailor advertisements based on individual preferences, past purchases, and browsing history. This level of personalization has further intensified the connection between shoppers and brands, influencing their decision-making processes and fueling spending habits.

As society evolves, so do consumer preferences and shopping trends. The advent of new technologies, such as artificial intelligence, virtual reality, and augmented reality, is reshaping the shopping experience. From personalized virtual showrooms to voice-activated purchases, these advancements are poised to revolutionize how we shop and spend in the future. Moreover, as sustainability and social responsibility become increasingly important to shoppers, businesses must adapt to meet these changing expectations.

The annual expenditure by shoppers in the world represents the cumulative impact of billions of individual choices and transactions. It is a testament to the power consumers hold in shaping economies, industries, and the future of commerce. Acknowledging the magnitude of our spending habits and understanding the broader implications allows us to make more informed decisions as consumers, leading to a more sustainable, equitable, and fulfilling global shopper's economy. By embracing conscious consumption, supporting ethical practices, and advocating for positive change, we can ensure that our spending contributes to a brighter and more inclusive future for all.

In an increasingly digital world, the opportunities for wealth creation have expanded beyond traditional brick-and-mortar businesses. The rise of the internet and technological advancements has paved the way for selling digital products, presenting individuals with a unique avenue to build wealth. In this chapter, we will explore the value of leveraging the digital frontier to create and sell digital products, empowering individuals to tap into a lucrative market and unlock their financial potential.

The advent of the internet has revolutionized the way we access and consume information, entertainment, and services. This digital revolution has democratized the playing field, enabling anyone with an internet connection to create, market, and sell digital products. Unlike physical goods, digital products exist in a non-tangible format, making them easily reproducible and accessible to a global audience at a low cost.

The market for digital products is vast and ever-growing, fueled by the increasing reliance on technology in our personal and professional lives. From e-books and online courses to software applications and digital artwork, the range of digital products is diverse, catering to a wide array of interests and needs. The scalability and potential for passive income inherent in selling digital products make it an attractive wealth-building strategy for entrepreneurs and creators alike.

One of the primary advantages of selling digital products is the minimal overhead costs involved. Unlike physical products that require manufacturing, inventory management, and shipping logistics, digital products can be created, stored, and delivered electronically. This eliminates the need for physical production, warehousing, and shipping, resulting in higher profit margins. Once the initial development and setup are complete, selling digital products becomes a largely automated and scalable process.

Digital products provide an avenue for individuals to monetize their expertise, skills, and creativity. Whether you are an industry expert, a talented artist, or a passionate teacher, selling digital products allows you to share your knowledge and creations with a global audience while generating income. By leveraging your unique talents and tapping into niche markets, you can create valuable digital products that resonate with your target audience and meet their specific needs.

The internet has transformed geographical boundaries into mere pixels on a screen, granting access to a vast global audience. Selling digital products eliminates the limitations of physical location, enabling entrepreneurs and creators to reach customers worldwide. Through effective digital marketing strategies, including search engine optimization, social media promotion, and targeted advertising, you can connect with individuals who are actively seeking the solutions, knowledge, or entertainment your digital products offer.

Building wealth often involves diversifying income streams to mitigate risks and create long-term stability. Selling digital products provides an opportunity to diversify your income sources, reducing reliance on a single revenue stream. By creating multiple digital products and optimizing their sales funnels, you can generate passive income, earning money even when you're not actively working. This passive income potential allows for greater financial freedom and flexibility.

The digital landscape is dynamic and ever-evolving, offering ample opportunities for growth and adaptability. Selling digital products enables you to stay agile and responsive to market trends and customer demands. As technology advances and new platforms emerge, you can leverage these developments to refine your digital products, expand your customer base, and stay ahead of the competition.

The digital revolution has unlocked a wealth of opportunities for individuals to create, market, and sell digital products, providing a path to financial independence and wealth building. The low overhead costs, global accessibility, and scalability of digital products make them an attractive asset for entrepreneurs and creators seeking to tap into the vast potential of the digital marketplace. By leveraging expertise, creativity, and digital marketing strategies, individuals can reach a global audience and generate income from their digital products.

Furthermore, selling digital products allows for diversification and the creation of passive income streams. By creating a portfolio of digital products, entrepreneurs can spread their risk and ensure a more stable income. With effective sales funnels and automated delivery systems, digital products can generate revenue even when the creator is not actively involved, providing the freedom to pursue other ventures or enjoy a flexible lifestyle.

The digital landscape is constantly evolving, presenting both challenges and opportunities. To succeed in selling digital products and building wealth, it is essential to stay adaptable and responsive to market trends. Regularly updating and improving digital products, exploring new distribution channels, and engaging with customers through feedback and market research are all vital steps in maintaining relevance and maximizing financial gains.

In addition to the financial benefits, selling digital products also offers intangible rewards. It provides a platform for individuals to share their knowledge, creativity, and passion with a global audience. Making a positive impact on people's lives, helping them solve problems or acquire new skills, can be deeply fulfilling and gratifying.

However, it is important to recognize that selling digital products requires effort, dedication, and strategic planning. Creating high-quality content, building an effective marketing strategy, and establishing a strong brand presence are essential steps in standing out in the competitive digital marketplace. Continuous learning, adapting to customer feedback, and refining product offerings are crucial for long-term success.

The value of selling digital products to build wealth lies in its potential for scalability, low overhead costs, and global accessibility. By leveraging expertise, creativity, and digital marketing strategies, individuals can tap into a vast marketplace and create diverse income streams. While the digital landscape presents opportunities, it also requires adaptability and continuous improvement. With dedication and a customer-centric approach, selling digital products can be a rewarding and lucrative path to wealth creation in the digital age.

When selling digital products, it is essential to protect your intellectual property rights. Copyright laws and licenses play a crucial role in safeguarding your creations from unauthorized use or distribution. By understanding and implementing proper copyright practices, such as watermarking, encryption, and licensing agreements, you can maintain control over your digital products and prevent infringement.

Selling digital products also opens doors for collaboration and affiliate partnerships. By teaming up with complementary creators or businesses, you can expand your reach and tap into new customer bases. Joint ventures, cross-promotions, and affiliate programs allow you to leverage each other's networks and benefit from shared marketing efforts, ultimately driving more sales and increasing revenue potential.

To maintain a competitive edge and sustain long-term success, it is vital to foster a culture of continuous innovation and product expansion. By staying attuned to market trends, customer feedback, and emerging technologies, you can identify opportunities to enhance your existing digital products or create new ones. Evolving and diversifying your product offerings not only attracts new customers but also keeps existing customers engaged, fostering loyalty and generating repeat business.

In the digital landscape, establishing a strong online presence is crucial for selling digital products successfully. Utilize various digital marketing channels, such as social media platforms, content marketing, search engine optimization (SEO), and email marketing, to build brand awareness and drive traffic to your digital product listings. Engage with your audience, provide valuable content, and build relationships to cultivate a loyal customer base.

Providing excellent customer support and engagement is paramount in the digital product selling journey. Promptly addressing customer inquiries, providing clear instructions, and ensuring a seamless purchasing experience enhances customer satisfaction and builds trust. Actively engaging with customers through social media, email newsletters, and forums fosters a sense of community and encourages positive word-of-mouth referrals.

Leveraging analytics and monitoring tools is essential for optimizing your digital product sales strategy. By tracking key performance indicators (KPIs) such as conversion rates, website traffic, and customer demographics, you gain insights into consumer behavior and can make data-driven decisions. These analytics enable you to refine your marketing tactics, target the right audience, and optimize your sales funnel for improved results.

Selling digital products provides a wealth-building opportunity with numerous advantages, including low overhead costs, scalability, and global accessibility. However, success in this arena requires strategic planning, continuous innovation, and a customer-centric approach. By protecting your intellectual property, collaborating with others, and building a strong online presence, you can maximize your potential for success. Embrace the digital frontier, adapt to market dynamics, and continuously improve your products and marketing efforts to harness the true value of selling digital products and pave the way to long-term wealth creation.

One of the remarkable aspects of selling digital products is the potential for scalability and automation. As the demand for your products grows, you can easily scale your operations without significant additional costs. With the right infrastructure in place, automated systems can handle product delivery, customer support, and transaction processing, allowing you to focus on creating and expanding your digital product offerings. This scalability and automation contribute to the potential for exponential growth and increased profitability.

Digital products offer the unique advantage of creating evergreen revenue streams. Unlike physical products that may require constant manufacturing or replenishment, digital products can be sold repeatedly without incurring additional production costs. Once you've created and launched a digital product, it can continue generating income for an extended period, making it a valuable asset for building long-term wealth.

In addition to standalone digital products, incorporating recurring subscription or membership models can further enhance your wealth-building potential. By offering exclusive access to premium content, ongoing updates, or a community of like-minded individuals, you can generate recurring revenue on a monthly or yearly basis. These models foster customer loyalty, ensure a steady income stream, and provide the opportunity for upselling or cross-selling additional products and services.

Diversifying your digital product formats can broaden your market reach and increase your revenue streams. For instance, if you primarily sell e-books, consider expanding into other formats such as online courses, video tutorials, templates, or software applications. By offering a range of products that cater to different preferences and learning styles, you can attract a wider audience and cater to various customer needs.

To amplify your digital product sales, consider collaborating with affiliates and influencers in your industry. Affiliates promote and recommend your products to their audience in exchange for a commission on sales generated. Influencers, with their large and engaged followings, can create buzz and drive interest in your digital products through sponsored content or reviews. These partnerships can significantly expand your reach, attract new customers, and boost your sales.

Marketing and promotion play a vital role in selling digital products. It's essential to have an ongoing marketing strategy to ensure consistent visibility and generate a steady stream of leads and sales. Utilize various digital marketing channels, including social media, content marketing, paid advertising, email marketing, and collaborations, to reach your target audience effectively. Regularly analyze and optimize your marketing efforts to maximize your return on investment and stay ahead of competitors.

Selling digital products provides an exciting opportunity to build wealth in the digital age. With scalability, automation, and the potential for recurring revenue, digital products offer a pathway to long-term financial success. By diversifying product formats, collaborating with affiliates and influencers, and continuously marketing and promoting your offerings, you can expand your reach, attract a global customer base, and unlock your wealth-building potential. Embrace the digital landscape, innovate, and adapt to changing market dynamics to harness the full value of selling digital products and pave your way to financial prosperity.

Take my client Alex for example. Alex had always been fascinated by technology and had a knack for creating digital products that solved real-world problems. While the city's residents went about their daily routines, Alex spent countless hours honing their skills in programming, graphic design, and content creation.

One day, inspired by the growing popularity of online marketplaces, Alex decided to embark on a journey to sell her digital creations to a global audience. With a humble laptop and unwavering determination, she set up an online store and carefully curated a collection of digital products that showcased her expertise and passion.

Her first product was an e-book that provided step-by-step instructions on mastering a complex software application. Alex poured her heart and soul into crafting a comprehensive guide that simplified the learning process. To her delight, the e-book gained popularity among individuals seeking to enhance their skills, and the positive reviews started pouring in.

Buoyed by the initial success, Alex ventured into creating online courses that catered to different skill levels and interests. With a charismatic teaching style and a talent for breaking down complex concepts into digestible modules, Alex's courses garnered a dedicated following. Students praised the quality of content, interactive exercises, and personalized feedback, spreading the word and attracting more learners.

As the demand for her digital products grew, Alex continued to innovate and diversify her offerings. She developed software applications that automated time-consuming tasks, designed beautifully crafted templates that streamlined workflow processes, and created stunning digital artwork that resonated with art enthusiasts around the world. Each product showcased

Alex's expertise and attention to detail, garnering recognition for their exceptional quality.

Word of Alex's digital products spread like wildfire, and soon she found herself receiving inquiries and partnership offers from influential industry figures and organizations. Collaborations with established brands and endorsements from respected experts further solidified Alex's reputation as a leading creator in their field.

With her newfound success, Alex made a conscious effort to give back to the community. She established scholarships and mentorship programs to help aspiring creators kickstart their own digital product businesses. Alex firmly believed that by nurturing talent and sharing knowledge, she could contribute to the growth and success of others.

Over time, Alex's online store transformed into a thriving business empire. Their digital products generated a steady stream of income, enabling her to live a life of financial freedom and pursue her passions. She traveled the world, attending conferences and giving keynote speeches, inspiring others with her journey and encouraging others to embrace the digital landscape.

Through hard work, dedication, and a commitment to excellence, Alex had achieved what seemed like an impossible dream. Her story became an inspiration for aspiring entrepreneurs and creators worldwide, showcasing the incredible potential of selling digital products online to build wealth and make a lasting impact.

In the fast-paced digital age we live in, there is no time like the present moment to embark on the journey of starting an online business. The internet has opened up a world of opportunities, empowering individuals to create and build their ventures with relative ease. In this chapter, we will explore the reasons why the present moment is the perfect time to launch your online business and take advantage of the ever-expanding digital landscape.

Unlike traditional brick-and-mortar businesses, starting an online business requires minimal barriers to entry. With a computer, an internet connection, and a small initial investment, anyone can establish their online presence and tap into a global market. The accessibility of online platforms, website builders, and e-commerce solutions has significantly reduced the costs and technical expertise required to launch a business, making it attainable for aspiring entrepreneurs of all backgrounds.

The digital economy is experiencing exponential growth, and its potential is far from being fully realized. The increasing reliance on technology, the rise of e-commerce, and the prevalence of digital services have created a fertile ground for online businesses to thrive. By leveraging the power of the internet, entrepreneurs can tap into this vast digital marketplace and reach customers around the globe. The potential customer base is virtually limitless, presenting immense growth opportunities for those willing to take the leap.

Consumer behavior has shifted dramatically in recent years, with more people embracing online shopping, digital services, and remote work. The convenience, variety, and accessibility of online businesses have resonated with consumers, who are increasingly turning to the internet for their purchasing decisions. By starting an online business now, you position yourself at the forefront of this changing landscape, catering to evolving consumer preferences and capitalizing on the growing demand for digital products and services.

Starting an online business allows for low-risk experimentation and testing of ideas. Unlike traditional businesses that often require significant upfront investments and long-term commitments, online businesses offer the flexibility to test different products, marketing strategies, and business models with relatively low financial risks. The ability to pivot, refine, and adapt based on real-time feedback from the market empowers entrepreneurs to fine-tune their offerings and maximize their chances of success.

The digital age has brought forth unparalleled marketing opportunities. Online businesses can leverage various digital marketing techniques, such as search engine optimization (SEO), social media marketing, content marketing, and influencer partnerships, to reach their target audience effectively. The ability to target specific demographics, track marketing metrics, and refine campaigns in real-time allows online businesses to optimize their marketing efforts and generate cost-effective results.

The rise of remote work and the growing acceptance of virtual collaboration have created an ideal environment for starting an online business. As businesses and individuals embrace remote work arrangements, the need for digital products and services that support remote work, enhance productivity, and enable seamless communication has surged. By tapping into this market, entrepreneurs can provide valuable solutions to remote workers and businesses alike, establishing themselves as leaders in the remote work ecosystem.

The present moment is characterized by rapid technological advancements and innovation. Emerging technologies such as artificial intelligence, blockchain, virtual reality, and the Internet of Things offer new avenues for online businesses to create groundbreaking products and services. By starting an online business now, you position yourself to leverage these emerging technologies, staying ahead of the curve and shaping the future of your industry.

There is no time like the present moment to launch your online business. The accessibility of online platforms, the rapidly growing digital economy, and the changing consumer behavior provide an environment rich with opportunities.

Affiliate Marketing

In the ever-evolving landscape of business, staying stagnant is no longer an option for sustainable growth. As a business owner or entrepreneur, you must constantly seek new avenues to expand your reach. In this chapter, we will explore the significance of expanding your reach and how it can fuel your business growth. By reaching out to new markets, demographics, and platforms, you can tap into untapped potential, open up new opportunities, and ensure long-term success.

Expanding your reach requires a growth mindset – a willingness to explore, adapt, and embrace change. By challenging your comfort zone and seeking new horizons, you position your business for progress and increased market presence.

Expanding your reach allows you to access new markets, both domestic and international. Diversifying your customer base mitigates the risk of overdependence on a single market and expands your revenue streams. Moreover, new markets often present unique needs and preferences that can inspire innovation and the development of new products or services.

Expanding your reach also involves connecting with previously untargeted demographics. Analyzing market research and consumer data can reveal potential customer segments that align with your offerings. By tailoring your marketing strategies and engaging these untapped demographics, you can broaden your customer base and establish brand loyalty among diverse audiences.

Expanding your reach inherently leads to increased revenue and profitability. With access to new markets and demographics, you can capture a larger share of the market and boost your sales. As your customer base grows, so does your potential for higher profits, economies of scale, and improved cash flow.

Expanding your reach enables you to amplify your brand's visibility and recognition. By tapping into new markets and demographics, you raise awareness about your products or services and build a stronger brand presence. This increased exposure helps establish your brand as a trusted and recognized player in the industry, enhancing your competitive advantage.

Expanding your reach diversifies your business and enhances its resilience. A broader customer base minimizes the impact of market fluctuations and reduces dependency on a single customer segment. By expanding across multiple markets, you can mitigate risks and adapt to changing market dynamics more effectively, ensuring your business remains robust and sustainable.

Conduct thorough market research to identify new opportunities and potential customer segments. Analyze consumer behavior, demographics, purchasing patterns, and emerging trends to tailor your offerings and marketing strategies effectively.

In the digital age, leveraging online platforms and channels is essential for expanding your reach. Establish a strong online presence through websites, social media, and e-commerce platforms to connect with a broader audience globally. Utilize digital marketing techniques such as search engine optimization (SEO), content marketing, and social media advertising to reach new customers.

Forge strategic collaborations and partnerships to extend your reach. Collaborating with complementary businesses or influencers can help access new customer segments and enhance brand exposure. Joint ventures, cross-promotions, and affiliate marketing programs are effective ways to tap into the existing networks of your partners and reach a wider audience.

Consider expanding your business geographically by opening new locations or entering new markets. Conduct thorough market analysis and evaluate the cultural, economic, and regulatory factors of the target region. Localize your offerings and marketing strategies to resonate with the new audience. This can involve setting up physical stores, distribution centers, or even exploring international markets through exports or partnerships with local distributors.

Continual innovation is key to expanding your reach. Analyze customer feedback, market trends, and emerging technologies to develop new products or services that cater to evolving needs. By offering unique and differentiated offerings, you can attract a wider customer base and stand out from competitors.

Active participation in industry events, conferences, and trade shows can significantly expand your reach. Networking with peers, industry experts, and potential customers opens doors to valuable connections and collaborations. These events provide opportunities to showcase your brand, build relationships, and gain insights into market trends and emerging opportunities.

Expanding your reach comes with its own set of challenges and risks. It requires careful planning, resource allocation, and adaptability. Here are some common challenges and strategies to address them:

Expanding your reach may require additional resources, such as capital, manpower, and infrastructure. Conduct a thorough assessment of your business capabilities and identify areas where you may need to invest or acquire resources to support expansion efforts.

Expanding into new markets, especially international ones, involves understanding cultural nuances and adapting your offerings and marketing strategies accordingly. Conduct market research, engage local experts, and build relationships with partners who have knowledge and experience in the target market.

Expanding your reach often means entering a more competitive landscape. Conduct a competitive analysis to understand the strengths and weaknesses of existing players. Differentiate your brand through unique value propositions, superior customer service, and continuous innovation.

Ensure that your business processes and operations can scale effectively to support expansion. Streamline workflows, invest in technology, and establish efficient supply chains to meet increased demand without compromising quality or customer experience.

Expanding your reach is a crucial strategy for sustainable business growth. By embracing new markets, demographics, and platforms, you can tap into untapped potential, increase revenue, enhance brand visibility, and establish business resilience. However, expanding your reach requires a growth mindset, thorough market research, strategic partnerships, digital presence, and continual innovation. By overcoming challenges and embracing opportunities, you can position your business for long-term success in a dynamic and competitive marketplace.

In the digital age, affiliate marketing has emerged as a powerful strategy for businesses to expand their reach, increase brand exposure, and drive revenue growth. In this chapter, we will explore the meaning of affiliate marketing, its core principles, and the potential it holds for businesses looking to leverage the power of partnerships and referrals.

Affiliate marketing is a performance-based marketing model where businesses reward affiliates for driving desired actions, such as generating sales, leads, or website traffic. Affiliates, also known as publishers or partners, promote the products or services of the advertiser (merchant) through various marketing channels and earn a commission for each successful referral or action.

The key players in affiliate marketing include the advertiser (merchant), affiliate (publisher), and the consumer. The advertiser provides the products or services, the affiliate promotes them, and the consumer makes a purchase or takes a specific action. Affiliate marketing relies on tracking technologies, unique referral links, and affiliate networks or platforms to facilitate and track the performance of affiliate campaigns.

Affiliates promote the advertiser's products or services through various marketing channels, such as their website, blog, social media, email newsletters, or video content. They incorporate unique affiliate links or banners provided by the advertiser, which track the referrals generated by the affiliate.

When a consumer clicks on an affiliate link and completes a desired action, such as making a purchase or submitting their contact information, the tracking technology captures and attributes the referral to the respective affiliate. This enables accurate measurement of conversions and determines the affiliate's commission.

Affiliate marketing operates on a commission-based model. The advertiser and affiliate agree upon a commission structure, which can be a percentage of the sale, a fixed amount per action, or a hybrid model. The commission rate varies based on factors like the industry, product type, and the value generated by the affiliate's efforts.

Affiliate networks or platforms act as intermediaries, connecting advertisers with potential affiliates. These networks provide a centralized platform for managing affiliate programs, tracking performance, facilitating payments, and enforcing compliance. Popular affiliate networks include Amazon Associates, ShareASale, and CJ Affiliate.

Affiliate marketing offers a cost-effective approach to marketing since businesses only pay affiliates for successful outcomes. Advertisers can allocate their marketing budget more efficiently and reduce the risk of investing in channels that do not yield results.

Through affiliate partnerships, businesses can tap into the existing audiences and networks of their affiliates. This allows for increased brand exposure, reaching potential customers who may not have been aware of the advertiser's products or services. Affiliate marketing facilitates access to niche markets and demographics, expanding the advertiser's reach beyond their immediate sphere of influence.

Affiliates often have established trust and credibility with their audience. When they endorse or recommend a product or service, it carries weight and influences consumer purchasing decisions. Affiliate marketing leverages this trust to enhance the advertiser's brand reputation and build customer confidence.

Affiliate marketing enables advertisers to track and measure the performance of their campaigns accurately. This data-driven approach allows for optimization, identifying top-performing affiliates and marketing channels. By focusing resources on high-converting affiliates, businesses can maximize their return on investment (ROI) and drive revenue growth.

Selecting the right affiliates is crucial for the success of an affiliate marketing program. Look for affiliates who align with your target audience, have relevant content or platforms, and possess a strong online presence. Additionally, consider their reputation, engagement levels, and track record of generating results in their previous partnerships.

Establish clear guidelines, expectations, and terms with your affiliates. Provide them with the necessary resources, such as promotional materials, product information, and tracking tools, to effectively promote your offerings. Maintain open lines of communication to address any questions, concerns, or updates promptly.

Motivate affiliates by offering attractive incentives and commission structures. Consider providing tiered commission rates based on performance levels, exclusive discounts or offers for their audience, or bonuses for surpassing specific targets. These incentives can incentivize affiliates to actively promote your products or services and drive higher conversions.

Implement robust tracking systems to accurately measure affiliate performance and conversions. Track key metrics such as clicks, conversions, average order value, and customer lifetime value. Leverage analytics to gain insights into affiliate performance, identify trends, optimize campaigns, and make data-driven decisions to improve overall program effectiveness.

Ensure that affiliates adhere to ethical marketing practices and comply with relevant regulations and guidelines. Monitor their promotional activities to maintain brand consistency and protect your brand reputation. Regularly review affiliate content and campaigns to ensure they align with your brand values and meet quality standards.

The rise of influencer marketing presents an opportunity to integrate affiliate marketing strategies. Collaborating with influencers can leverage their influential reach, audience engagement, and storytelling capabilities to drive affiliate sales and expand brand visibility.

With the increasing prevalence of mobile devices, optimizing affiliate marketing for mobile platforms is crucial. Ensure that affiliate links, landing pages, and tracking mechanisms are mobile-friendly for a seamless user experience and higher conversion rates.

Attributing conversions accurately across multiple marketing channels is a growing challenge in affiliate marketing. Developing advanced attribution models and utilizing technologies like multi-touch attribution can provide a more comprehensive understanding of the customer journey and fairly attribute conversions to affiliate efforts.

Artificial intelligence (AI) technologies can enhance affiliate marketing by automating processes, analyzing data at scale, and optimizing campaigns in real-time. AI-powered tools can help identify high-performing affiliates, predict consumer behavior, and deliver personalized experiences to maximize conversions.

Affiliate marketing is a dynamic and effective strategy for businesses to expand their reach, increase brand exposure, and drive revenue growth. By leveraging partnerships, tracking performance, and incentivizing affiliates, businesses can tap into new markets, enhance credibility, and optimize their marketing efforts. As technology evolves and new trends emerge, affiliate marketing continues to evolve, offering exciting opportunities for businesses to forge valuable partnerships and achieve long-term success.

In today's digital landscape, affiliate marketing has become a powerful tool for online businesses to generate revenue, increase brand visibility, and expand their customer base. In this chapter, we will explore the compelling reasons why you should consider incorporating affiliate marketing into your online business strategy.

One of the most significant advantages of affiliate marketing is its cost-effectiveness. Traditional marketing methods often involve substantial upfront costs, such as advertising fees, production expenses, and ongoing maintenance. With affiliate marketing, you only pay commissions to affiliates when they successfully drive desired actions, such as sales or leads. This performance-based model allows you to allocate your marketing budget efficiently and maximize your return on investment.

Affiliate marketing provides a valuable opportunity to tap into new markets and reach a wider audience. By partnering with affiliates who have established online platforms, you can leverage their existing reach and influence. Affiliates introduce your products or services to their audience, attracting potential customers who may not have been aware of your business. This expanded reach helps increase brand exposure, drive traffic to your website, and boost conversions.

Affiliates often have a trusted relationship with their audience, built over time through their expertise, authenticity, and valuable content. When affiliates endorse your products or services, their followers perceive it as a recommendation from a trusted source. This endorsement enhances your brand's credibility and instills trust in potential customers, leading to higher conversion rates and customer loyalty.

Acquiring new customers can be an expensive and time-consuming process. With affiliate marketing, you can leverage the networks and efforts of affiliates to acquire customers more cost-effectively. Affiliates act as an extension of your sales force, promoting your offerings and driving targeted traffic to your website. By paying commissions based on performance, you only invest in acquiring customers when they convert, making it a highly efficient customer acquisition strategy.

Affiliate marketing provides valuable insights and data that can inform your marketing decisions. Through tracking technologies and analytics, you gain visibility into the performance of your affiliate campaigns. You can measure key metrics such as clicks, conversions, and customer behavior, allowing you to optimize your marketing efforts, identify top-performing affiliates, and refine your target audience. This data-driven approach enables you to make informed decisions to maximize the effectiveness of your affiliate marketing program.

Affiliate marketing offers scalability and flexibility, making it suitable for businesses of all sizes. Whether you're a small startup or an established enterprise, you can adapt your affiliate program to align with your business goals and resources. You have the flexibility to set commission rates, adjust promotional strategies, and scale the program based on your business needs. As your business grows, you can onboard more affiliates and expand into new markets, leveraging the scalability of the affiliate marketing model.

Through affiliate marketing, you have the opportunity to form strategic partnerships with affiliates who align with your brand values and target audience. These partnerships extend beyond transactional relationships, enabling you to collaborate on content creation, joint promotions, and cross-marketing initiatives. By nurturing these partnerships, you can unlock synergistic opportunities, amplify your brand's reach, and foster long-term business growth.

In today's competitive online landscape, affiliate marketing can provide a significant competitive advantage. By incorporating this marketing strategy, you can differentiate your business from competitors, especially if they are not utilizing affiliates. Affiliate marketing allows you to tap into unique marketing channels, access niche audiences, and leverage the trusted voices of influencers within your industry. This advantage can help you stand out, increase market share, and establish

Integrating affiliate marketing into your online business diversifies your revenue streams. Instead of relying solely on direct sales or advertising, you can generate income through affiliate commissions. This additional revenue source provides stability and reduces the risk of overdependence on a single income stream. By diversifying your revenue, you create a more sustainable and resilient business model.

Affiliate marketing offers the potential for continuous growth and adaptability. As you onboard new affiliates and expand your network, your reach and customer base can expand exponentially. Moreover, the affiliate marketing landscape is dynamic, with new trends, technologies, and affiliate opportunities emerging regularly. By staying informed and adapting your strategies, you can harness these opportunities to drive ongoing growth and stay ahead of the competition.

Incorporating affiliate marketing into your online business can bring numerous benefits and opportunities for growth. From cost-effective marketing and expanded reach to improved credibility and strategic partnerships, affiliate marketing offers a versatile and scalable approach to driving revenue and increasing brand visibility. By leveraging the power of affiliates, you can tap into new markets, acquire customers efficiently, and build a thriving online business. Embrace affiliate marketing as a strategic component of your marketing strategy and position your business for long-term success in the digital era.

Scaling Up

In the ever-changing landscape of business, the importance of planning for long-term growth cannot be overstated. While short-term objectives are crucial for immediate success, a well-thought-out long-term growth strategy ensures the sustainability and prosperity of a business in the future. This chapter delves into the significance of long-term planning, highlighting its benefits and offering practical insights for entrepreneurs and business leaders.

Long-term growth planning begins with visionary thinking. It involves envisioning where you want your business to be in the coming years and setting ambitious yet achievable goals. By having a clear vision, you provide direction for your company, inspire your team, and create a framework for decision-making. A compelling vision serves as a roadmap, guiding your business through challenges and opportunities.

Long-term growth planning enables businesses to build sustainable competitive advantage. This involves identifying and developing unique strengths and capabilities that differentiate your organization from competitors. Whether it's through technological innovation, superior customer service, or operational efficiency, sustainable competitive advantage allows businesses to thrive in a crowded marketplace and establish themselves as industry leaders.

The business environment is dynamic, characterized by rapid technological advancements, shifting customer preferences, and evolving market trends. Long-term growth planning helps businesses anticipate and adapt to these changes effectively. By conducting market research, staying informed about industry trends, and regularly reviewing and updating your growth strategy, you can pivot your business, seize emerging opportunities, and mitigate risks.

Long-term growth planning encourages businesses to nurture a culture of innovation and continuous improvement. By allocating resources and fostering an environment that encourages creativity, experimentation, and learning, organizations can stay ahead of the curve. Embracing innovation not only helps businesses develop new products or services but also enhances operational efficiency, customer satisfaction, and overall competitiveness.

An effective long-term growth plan can significantly contribute to attracting and retaining top talent. Employees seek opportunities for growth and development, and businesses that demonstrate a commitment to long-term success are more likely to attract high-performing individuals. A clear growth strategy also allows for succession planning and talent management, ensuring a smooth transition of leadership roles and fostering a sense of stability within the organization.

Planning for long-term growth provides businesses with a solid foundation for securing financial stability and attracting investments. Investors and financial institutions are more inclined to support organizations that have a well-defined growth plan and a track record of executing strategic initiatives. Additionally, long-term planning enables businesses to manage financial risks, allocate resources efficiently, and make informed decisions about capital investments.

Long-term growth planning ultimately aims to create value for stakeholders. By setting and achieving long-term goals, businesses not only generate profits but also contribute to the broader community and society. A sustainable and successful business positively impacts employees, customers, suppliers, and the local economy. Moreover, by aligning the interests of stakeholders with the company's growth strategy, businesses can foster long-term partnerships and loyalty.

Planning for long-term growth is an essential aspect of building a successful and sustainable business. It provides direction, adaptability, and a competitive edge in an ever-changing market. By embracing visionary thinking, nurturing innovation, attracting top talent, and securing financial stability, businesses can navigate challenges, seize opportunities, and create long-lasting value for stakeholders. A well-crafted long-term growth strategy serves as a roadmap, guiding businesses towards a prosperous future.

Long-term growth planning helps businesses align their resources and priorities effectively. By setting clear objectives and identifying the necessary resources to achieve them, organizations can allocate their time, money, and talent efficiently. This alignment ensures that all efforts are focused on activities that contribute to long-term growth, eliminating wasted resources and increasing overall productivity.

The business landscape is fraught with risks and uncertainties that can impact growth. Long-term planning allows businesses to identify potential risks and develop strategies to mitigate them. By conducting thorough risk assessments and scenario planning, organizations can anticipate challenges and put measures in place to minimize their impact. This proactive approach provides a sense of stability and resilience, even in turbulent times.

Long-term growth planning places a strong emphasis on building and enhancing customer relationships. Businesses that prioritize long-term success invest in understanding their customers' needs, preferences, and behaviors. By incorporating customer feedback into their growth strategy, organizations can tailor their products, services, and marketing efforts to meet evolving customer demands. This customer-centric approach fosters loyalty, attracts new customers through positive word-of-mouth, and drives sustainable growth.

A well-executed long-term growth plan enables businesses to expand their market presence. Whether through geographic expansion, diversification of product offerings, or targeting new customer segments, businesses that plan for long-term growth position themselves for strategic expansion. This expansion not only increases market share but also creates opportunities for economies of scale, improved bargaining power, and enhanced competitiveness.

Long-term growth planning encourages businesses to seek strategic partnerships that can fuel their growth trajectory. Collaborating with complementary businesses, suppliers, or technology partners can provide access to new markets, resources, and expertise. Strategic partnerships offer the opportunity to leverage each other's strengths, share risks, and capitalize on synergies, ultimately driving accelerated growth.

A long-term growth plan is not a static document but rather a living roadmap that requires regular monitoring and iteration. Businesses must track their progress against predetermined milestones, key performance indicators (KPIs), and financial targets. This allows for course correction and adjustment of strategies as needed. By continuously evaluating and updating the growth plan, businesses can stay agile and responsive to changing circumstances, ensuring long-term success.

Effective long-term growth planning involves transparent and consistent communication with stakeholders. By sharing the growth vision, strategy, and progress updates, businesses can align their employees, investors, and other stakeholders towards a common goal. Transparent communication fosters trust, motivates employees, and creates a sense of shared purpose, which is crucial for driving long-term growth.

Planning for long-term growth is a strategic imperative for businesses that aspire to thrive in a competitive marketplace. By aligning resources, mitigating risks, enhancing customer relationships, expanding market presence, fostering partnerships, and tracking progress, businesses can chart a path towards sustainable and meaningful growth. A well-executed long-term growth plan not only drives financial success but also creates a lasting impact on employees, customers, and the broader community. Embrace the power of long-term planning and set your business on a trajectory of enduring success.

Long-term growth planning necessitates embracing innovation and disruption as key drivers of success. In today's rapidly evolving business landscape, industries are constantly being reshaped by technological advancements and changing customer expectations. Businesses that prioritize long-term growth actively seek out opportunities to innovate and disrupt traditional practices. They invest in research and development, foster a culture of creativity, and explore new technologies and business models to stay ahead of the curve. By embracing innovation, businesses can unlock untapped potential, differentiate themselves from competitors, and seize new growth avenues.

In the era of big data, long-term growth planning relies heavily on leveraging data and analytics. Businesses that adopt data-driven decision-making have a competitive edge. They gather and analyze market data, customer insights, and performance metrics to gain a comprehensive understanding of their business landscape. This data-driven approach enables businesses to identify trends, make informed strategic choices, and optimize their operations for maximum growth. By harnessing the power of data, businesses can unlock valuable insights that fuel long-term success.

Long-term growth planning requires businesses to consider regulatory and environmental factors. Regulations and laws can significantly impact industry practices, market access, and competitive dynamics. Businesses that proactively monitor and adapt to regulatory changes position themselves for sustainable growth. Additionally, embracing environmental sustainability is not just a corporate social responsibility but also a strategic imperative. By incorporating sustainable practices into their long-term growth plan, businesses can mitigate risks, enhance their brand reputation, and tap into emerging green markets.

Successful long-term growth planning involves anticipating customer needs and market trends. Businesses must stay attuned to evolving customer preferences, emerging technologies, and market shifts. By conducting market research, monitoring consumer behavior, and engaging in trend analysis, organizations can stay ahead of the curve and identify opportunities for innovation and growth. Anticipating and meeting customer needs proactively not only ensures customer satisfaction but also fosters customer loyalty and drives long-term business growth.

While long-term growth planning focuses on future success, it is essential to strike a balance with short-term results. Businesses must navigate the delicate equilibrium between short-term performance and long-term vision. Short-term wins provide the financial stability and momentum necessary for sustained growth. However, it is crucial not to sacrifice long-term objectives for short-term gains. Successful businesses prioritize both short-term profitability and long-term strategic initiatives to build a solid foundation for continuous growth and success.

Long-term growth planning is an iterative process that requires continuous learning and adaptation. The business landscape is dynamic, and strategies that were effective in the past may not yield the same results in the future. Businesses must remain agile and adaptable, willing to learn from their experiences and make necessary adjustments. By fostering a culture of continuous learning, businesses can embrace change, seize new opportunities, and continuously refine their growth strategies to stay competitive and relevant.

ABOUT THE AUTHOR

Dr. Jeremy Lopez is Founder and President of Identity Network and Now Is Your Moment. Identity Network is one of the world's leading prophetic resource sites, offering books, teachings, and courses to a global audience. For more than thirty years, Dr. Lopez has been considered a pioneering voice within the field of the prophetic arts and his proven strategies for success coaching are now being implemented by various training groups and faith groups throughout the world. Dr. Lopez is the author of more than forty books, including his international bestselling books The Universe is at Your Command and Creating with Your Thoughts. Throughout his career, he has spoken prophetically into the lives of heads of business as well as heads of state. He has ministered to Governor Bob Riley of the State of Alabama, Prime Minister Benjamin Netanyahu, and Shimon Peres. Dr. Lopez continues to be a highly sought conference teacher and host, speaking on the topics of human potential and spirituality.

www.ingramcontent.com/pod-product-compliance
Lightning Source LLC
Chambersburg PA
CBHW070927260726
48661CB00003B/854